A Black Man's Notes on

Ancient Egypt

BY KARL C. PIERCE

Dorrance Publishing Co
585 Alpha Drive
Suite 103
Pittsburgh, PA 15238
Visit our website at *www.dorrancebookstore.com*

ISBN: 979-8-89341-702-9
eISBN: 979-8-89027-672-8

Table of Contents

Introduction

While in college many years ago studying for an Urban Planning Degree, I took a class dealing with the "History of Planning." This class was focused on early human civilizations concerning the planning, functionality and vitality of early villages, towns, and cities.

During the early weeks of the class, we studied ancient civilizations. European books and colleges teach that the Fertile Crescent (Iran/Iraq) is where "civilization" began along the Tigris and Euphrates Rivers nearly 7,000 years ago. Thus, this is where our studies began. I was a bit troubled by this notion concerning the origins of civilizations, and since I knew a little something about early Africa, I asked my professor, "What about Africa?"

His response was, "We just don't know that much about Africa." Then he moved on, casually brushing me aside, just as European scholars have ignored and dismissed Africa for centuries.

Yet, this was particularly disturbing because, at the time, the University (San José State) had a Black Studies Program in the same department, literally just a few feet away from the Urban Studies professors' offices. My professor could have easily walked a few feet down the hall to ask those black professors about early/ancient African civilizations, yet he chose not to do so. European/American scholars at that time gave no serious consideration toward, nor acknowledgment of, African historical and/or cultural contributions. They viewed people in Africa as uncivilized savages, so certainly these savages could not have had anything to contribute towards a *civilized society*. These scholars were generally not interested in learning about Africa, either; therefore, they were dismissive and/or ignorant of Africa's vast rich history.

My first remembrance of questions about my African heritage is when Malcom X told the Black masses that we, *Black people*, are from a nation of "Kings and Queens"—Africa, and specifically Egypt. Today the European world continues to tell us that we are from slaves, second-class people. Malcom's message was that Black Africans/Egyptians, Ethiopians, Nubians, and others were adorned with gold and silks and resided in vibrant cities while white folks (Europeans) still resided in caves. Malcolm's revelations may sound like a lot of "hype," created in support of Black pride, but history proves and validates the truth of his words. For much of Black America, his statements were an awakening! At this time, Blacks as a group were not well traveled and had not yet read about, or seen the thousands of Black images, paintings, and monuments of Ancient Egypt and Africa. Europeans have taught us for generations their white, slanted view of history—that Black Africans are, and have always been, savages. In fact, a large percentage of white society today still treat Blacks as second-class people. Because of Malcolm's words, I started looking into my own history, my African history.

The Autobiography of Malcolm X was one of the first books I read of my own initiative. This was a time of racial turbulence, and an awakening for Blacks in America. Like most young Black men, I was terribly upset with the daily doses of discrimination and disrespect of black folks by white society. So, Malcolm's words, in a way, clicked on a switch in my mind and spurred me to look deeper into this subject. Malcolm's bold, unapologetic Black voice shouted that, "The white man was lying to us," and "We should study our own history." He had piqued my interest. This is when I started my own investigation, searching for black scholars.

Early on in this process while channel surfing on television I ran across (unknown to me) noted Black scholar Dr. John Henrik Clarke giving a symposium on his work, *A Great and Mighty Walk*. After listening to him, I was *all in!* The following pages represent my notes from various readings on the subject. I, basically, started my studies as a hobby. I am not a scholar on the subject, just an individual who sought some deeper knowledge on my true history. In what follows, I will lay out simple, straight-forward explanations of what my research revealed. Hopefully, I will answer some of the prevalent questions you may have about Egypt and Africa.

I have tried to write this for the average person to easily consume. I do not delve into a deep comprehensive study of Egyptian history; it is far too complicated for me and this work. There are many wonderful books available by noted scholars on the subject. I sight a few at the end of this writing that helped me along. Hopefully, you will find these pages worthwhile reading.

Perhaps this can aid you in questioning/searching your own history. I invite you to do your own research and to ask your own questions. It will be an eye-opening experience. Black folks are an extremely spiritual and religious peoples. If you hold certain religious convictions, some of this information may be contrary to your beliefs, as some of this historic and scientific material may be difficult to reconcile with your Bible. But I ask that you keep an open mind. Ask yourself some simple questions: Where do you come from? Who are your ancestors? What really is your beginning? Today, researching your ancestry is popular across all ethnic groups, resulting in a new multibillion-dollar industry. Each of us owes it to ourselves to look deeper to understand our own African heritage beyond *American history* and DNA readings. I ask that you look deeper into your ancestor's history as a people, their origins, culture, and accomplishments.

**Note: To steer clear of any copyright issues the photos taken in this book were taken by me on a recent trip to Egypt. In some cases, it will be helpful for the reader to have a visual of historical persons or places. If my photos are not sufficient , I ask the reader to pause at that moment (or later), go to the internet to pull up an image of those persons or places cited that may be better illustrations.*

Africa—Origin Of Mankind

Noted Physical Anthropologist and Professor Louis Leakey established in 1971 through fossil findings (*OMO-1 skull* in *Ethiopia*) that today's *modern humans* (homo sapiens sapiens) initially evolved and lived in Africa approximately 250,000 to 300,000 years ago. These findings are now accepted at all scholarly levels of science. The term Homo-sapiens (wise man) refers to early man. There were originally 10 to 14 human relatives that developed at different periods in mankind's early existence. Today, there is fossil and DNA evidence of up to 24 different species. All these species developed originally in Africa. Of these, Lucy, found by Paleoanthropologist Dr. Donald Johanson in 1974, is perhaps the oldest and the best known to the average person. Scientists date her remains to 3.5 million years ago. Lucy's remains, found in Ethiopia, continue to be the most complete set of fossil remains of man's earliest *human* relative, although she was not considered Homo, but designated a relative. Of all these early human relatives, *at least three* survived to travel outside of Africa: Homo Erectus (*up right* walking man: 800,000 – 1,000,000 yrs. ago), Homo Neanderthals (400,000 yrs. ago) and finally Homo Sapiens Sapiens. We distinguish modern man from Neanderthals, etc., as a subspecies by the designation of Homo-sapiens-sapiens. Of all these early Homo species, only one—modern man (Homo-sapiens-sapiens)—has survived to this day; all others are now extinct.

As stated, Lucy and a few other early relatives were not called homo species. Science calls her species Australopithecus, but her remains have been linked to modern humans. Her remains (surprisingly, discovered lying on the *surface* of the ground) are not exactly in the likeness of modern-day man, but she was anatomically (bone/body structure) the same, certifying our earliest relatives. Additionally, it has been since determined and verified by science that there is NO evidence of any other Homo-sapiens species ever developing outside of Africa. It is now accepted fact that the *first* humans developed in Africa, before migrating throughout Africa and into other regions of the world (see Exhibit A). It is my view that outdated and inaccurate high school course material covering this subject clearly needs to be updated and clarified. You probably recall a graphic from science class depicting a series of 10 or more figures representing these early relatives/Hominins. These figures begin with a likeness of an ape-like creature, then a "Lucy" type (an upright walker), and finally ends with modern man, Homo sapiens-sapiens, shown in most cases a WHITE MAN. This is NOT true! The first modern anatomical humans on earth were Black; and remained black for thousands of years. Johanson's book, *Lucy*, is one of the few times it appears to be a Black man shown at the end of that Homo chain. We will discuss this more later in this book.

You might ask, what were the factors that designated Lucy as the first *anatomical human?* From the fossil remains found in East Africa, physical anthropologists were able to prove Lucy's connection to modern man. Lucy was about three feet tall, perhaps 60 pounds, and thus much smaller than today's typical human. But a few of the telling features that put Lucy in the human category are 1) upright walking (*bipedal*); 2) straight big toes (*unlike curved, spaced big toes critical for tree climbing by her predecessors*); 3) longer legs (to better traverse new open Savanah's because of climate changes), and shorter arms. The longer legs were better suited for pursuing game and escaping danger.

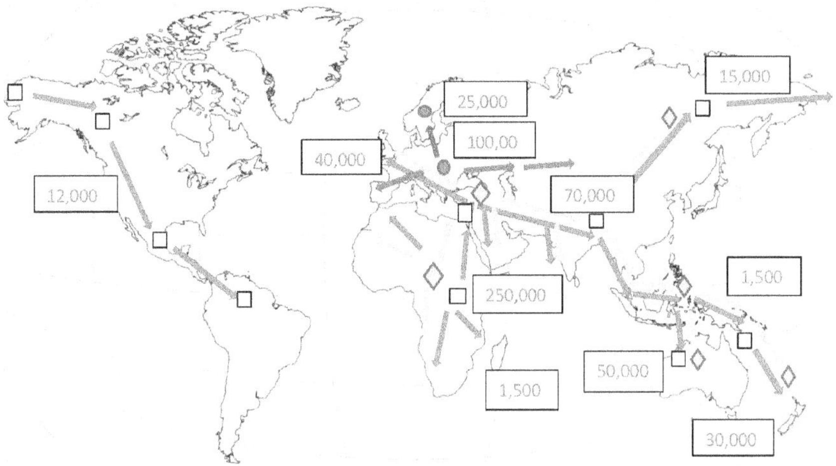

Exhibit A : Estimated Early Hominin Migration Out of Africa

Homo Sapiens Sapiens : 1st Appeared 200,000 – 300,000 Yrs. Ago

Homo Neanderthals: Appeared 400,000 – 500,000 Yrs. Ago

Homo Erectus: Appeared 800,000 –1,000,000 Yrs. Ago

EXHIBIT A : ESTIMATED EARLY HOMININ MIGRATION OUT OF AFRICA

4) the jawbone and type of teeth, which are *much different than that of apes*; and 5) the round skull and larger brain sizes were critically important factors in later human development. Since Lucy, anthropologists have discovered another human species thought to be 1 million years older than Lucy; she is called Ardi. Interestingly, humans and chimpanzees are 99% similar in DNA. Now, new, and perhaps the earliest human relative fossils have been recently found in Kenya called Orrorin Tugensis also known as Millennium Man – dated to 6.2 million years old.

In 1901 there was some European (white) excitement in the discovery of a set of human bones found in Italy that dated to be 30,000 years old—a modern man, Homo-sapiens-sapiens (he was called Grimaldi man). This was thought to be proof of an ancient European (white) human originating on European soil. But scientific study, genetics, and DNA testing found that these bones were from a sub-Saharan (African) individual(s), further validating and reinforcing the ONE source (monogenetic development) of modern man—that being Africa. Grimaldi man was called *Grimaldi Negro* by some scholars. It was later determined that it was two sets of bones, not one. For some unknown reason, Africa—and only Africa—had the right environment and natural setting for the development of the human species. As such, Blacks existed thousands of years before the white man appeared. **This is established, accepted science and is no longer open for debate by any credible scientific theory.** There was one other case called *Piltdown Man* thought to be a European early man. It took 50 years before it was discovered to be an elaborate fraud. Johanson would later call Africa *"the cradle of humanity."* Noted black Egyptologist Dr. C.A. Diop, in his explanation of the African origins of the human species, believes that this was and is an unexplained scientific occurrence. He further opined that we, as Black people, should not assume any sort of *"chosen people" story line.* He believes that: *"Nature, science, and the environment simply ran its course."*

I mentioned Lucy was not of the homo species, but she was a hominin. To further clarify, although many Homo species have been identified, the primary five are as follows:

1. Australopithecus Africanus (Lucy - aka, Southern ape)
2. Homo Habilis – (aka, Handy man)
3. Homo Erectus – (aka, Upright man)
4. Homo Sapiens (Neanderthal – aka Wise man)
5. Homo Sapiens Sapiens (aka, - doubly Wise man)

If you accept the science, the human species starting with Lucy and Ardi has been on earth for millions of years. These early relatives once shared a common ancestry with apes, but even more millions of years earlier a split occurred in the species, which eventually led to a divergent path of development of Lucy and Homo Sapiens. Modern man has been on earth in Africa for 250,000 to 300,000 years. Egypt, located in northern Africa, is considered the first great human civilization—it being at least 10,000 years old, even though man has resided in the Nile Valley for perhaps 20,000 to 30,000 years prior. According to science, modern humans have been here for thousands of years, but today we just do not think in terms of *thousands of years*. Yet these are the actual timelines that we will deal with in this book, revealing the historic truths about Africa and human existence. As we go forward, I will continue to point to dates and offer timelines that should help to organize and familiarize the reader with important events of ancient Egypt.

First, let us quickly revisit this term "sub-Saharan." Please understand that this term was created by whites/Europeans as a tool to delegitimize Black African's contributions to the world. Dr. Rebecca Futo Kennedy, a professor at Denison University and director of the Denison Museum, is an expert in Antiquity Studies. She is featured in a YouTube educational symposium, "Antiquity and the Middle Ages—Herodotus on Ancient Africa." During this symposium, she highlights a graph that she prepared which demonstrates that the term "sub-Saharan" was rarely used until late in the twentieth century, about 1980. The graph shows usage of that term at an almost flat line for decades, when in around 1980, that flat line started trending upward. It then spiked almost straight up where it has remained constant every year since and is now a commonly used term by educators and political interests. Of course, the implication here is that people north of the Sahara Desert today are designated as Semitic, Arab or European, with few Blacks, while those below the Sahara, "*sub-Saharan*" people, are by implication 100 percent Black.

Dr. Kennedy makes it clear that this *new* term was utilized primarily by doubters to support a belief or narrative that in ancient times Black people were not in Egypt, because they exist primarily below the Sahara Desert; therefore, Egyptians were white, or anything but Black. This is false!

Science and history show that in ancient times the climate in the area was quite different. Egypt was not primarily a desert as we know it today. Also, in the 16th thru 19th centuries, vast numbers of Africans fled from the north, south into the *interior of the continent* to escape the changing climate, the constant threat of European incursions and the continuing danger of slave traders. So "sub-Saharan" is, basically, another European construct to take Black Africans out of North Africa. Dr. Kennedy says it is laughable to say that Ancient Egyptians were not African.

The Truth About Africa

First, let us establish that Africa is earth's second largest continent, and has perhaps the richest accumulation of mineral resources and raw materials of any continent — gold, diamonds, ivory, platinum, uranium, cobalt, rubber, coco, oil, etc. At one time, scientists estimated that the continent of Africa had perhaps 30-40% of the world's entire valuable mineral resources. These natural resources, just like the African people, have been exploited in the past and are still being exploited today. One familiar example of this is the cell phone and battery industries. These industries are largely possible because of precious "rare earth minerals" found in great quantities in Africa. Today, "Big Tech," plus other businesses and their suppliers, have established corporate control and continue to rape Africa by extracting resources. When local people try desperately to benefit from this gold mine of resources in their land big business is there to take advantage of this ridiculously cheap labor by poor Africans, including children. These minerals are used for nuclear power, semi-conductors, batteries, etc. Other large industries, including diamond mines, chocolate companies, and the rubber industry, all depend to a large degree on African resources for their successes, while most African people remain stuck in shocking poverty.

One line of thought by some economists is that the global economic structure needs Africa to *stay poor.* Numerous old one-sided colonial agreements still handcuff African progress. African uranium from Niger, for example, fuels

France's nuclear power plants and lights up the city of Paris to this very day! France is perhaps the most egregious European country in this regard since historically, 14 African countries were under its colonial domination. These 14 countries still speak French and to large degree still use France's currency, which makes them today still heavily dependent on French banks, and, thus, the French government.

To crystalize this point, we have only to listen to the words of former French Prime Minister Jacques Chirac (1932-2019). Out of his mouth the following words make clear Frances's deliberate underdevelopment of African countries. In a January 24, 2001, edition of the magazine/paper *Canard* he said:

"While regarding Africa, we must check our memory. We (the French) started draining the continent four hundred and fifty years ago with the slave trade. Next, we discovered their raw materials and seized them. Having deprived Africans of their wealth, we sent our elites who destroyed their culture. There upon we are claiming that the unfortunate Africa is not in a brilliant condition and is not making elites. Having enriched on its back, we are now lecturing?"

Chirac, in this case found himself being brutally honest (after a couple of cocktails loosened his tongue) in defending Africa against a French religious cleric who was demeaning African progress. Chirac's statement, can rightfully, be applied to all European countries and their roles in Africa's continued undeveloped condition.

Africa has been prevented from establishing any manufacturing base. Africa relies heavily on exporting its natural resources to the world, but this is not sustainable as an economic driver because prices are up and down over the years, so the African economy, in general, continues to struggle. This line of thought suggests a manufacturing base is the best way forward for Africa. Manufacturing would allow Africa to prosper on its own terms. But the world economic and political structure will not allow this. Imagine Africa mining, processing, manufacturing, and distributing products from its own natural resources to the world! This would be an economic game changer! Yet, this is not possible, as shrewd foreign powers cut sweet deals for themselves with the help of some past corrupt African leaders, thus gaining control of in-country natural resources. This allowed some past African leaders to become enormously wealthy, while local peoples remain destitute. Today, we can add China to the list of those outside nations aggressively seeking African land and resources as their own population grows.

Historically, Europeans have subjugated, enslaved, and murdered Africans by the millions. They arrived on distant virgin shores searching for gold and riches. The import of Christianity also has had an enormous negative impact on what Europeans called *"pagan"* peoples and their lands. Whites came to Africa initially posing as friends and trading partners, but soon were moving to take control of the indigenous peoples and natural resources. In this way, Europeans first posing as friends, tricked, then betrayed trusting African people. They later aggressively bullied their way into Africa, taking *by force* its resources, murdering and enslaving its peoples.

Europeans have routinely robbed indigenous peoples around the globe and taken their land, particularly during the massive colonization period of 1400 to 1800. The final step in establishing control over these indigenous peoples was by converting them to their European religions, Christianity in most cases, this by coercion, or force. Historically religion has always been a primary tool used by the elite, upper class for *controlling* populations. During this period of colonization, the European GOD was introduced and imposed throughout Africa. Africans were made to worship this god—the very same GOD who eventually allowed them to be murdered and over-run by their European conquerors. Dr. John Henrik Clarke said, *"Europeans came as guests, then stayed as conquerors. At the outset Africans were unfamiliar, and sometimes afraid of this ghostly white man, and thus naïve to the European's ultimate plan for them."*

European countries—England, Spain, France, Portugal, etc.,—were in constant competition for resources and power. In the 1300 and 1400's, these same countries had been devastated economically due to famine, plague, etc., and were thrust deeply into their *Dark Ages*. It is estimated that one-third of the entire European population (100-150 million) died from the "Black Plague." They suffered terribly because of crowded cities, poor hygiene, limited access to land and resources, including food. There was a desperate need to quickly find new resources for its struggling economies. It is interesting to note that during this same period, Africa was a land of plenty. It is documented that the legendary King of Mali, Mansa Musa, was the richest man on earth then, and possibly of all time (he was worth an estimated Four Hundred billion in today's dollars). So, in need of food and other resources to survive, Europeans, by necessity, had to search outside of Europe. Gold, as usual, was always at the top of their list, and they had heard for years the stories of Africa's riches.

So came the age of European discovery, and as a result, the age of murder, terror, and colonization worldwide. Outside of the Americas, Africa was by far the biggest prize. As mentioned, Europeans had heard the tales of African wealth, and eagerly sought her resources. Europeans began to pillage and ravage Africa during this period. The colonization process and racism would negatively impact Africa's future for hundreds of years to come. The Portuguese were the first of many European countries to enter Africa in search of trade and riches. According to historians, voyages to Africa and the New World produced heavily armed ships traversing the seas filled with mercenaries and criminals—*not men of good will*. It was primarily these types of characters who joined these dangerous voyages. These folks had no problem with forcefully moving in, raping, killing, and subduing entire populations. *At some critical point, these invaders calculated that enslaving people would be far more profitable than just sending back pilfered goods to their homelands.* Every European country eagerly sought their slice of the African pie, which included turning local peoples into slaves as human bounty.

To facilitate this plunder of Africa, the Berlin Conference (Congo Conference) 1884–1885 was convened by Europeans. With *not one* African present, they went about a process of carving up the entire African continent amongst themselves. This conference was held to prevent these various "*Christian countries*" from warring against each other over resource rich Africa. They eventually forcefully imposed and designated/drew boundary lines for each African country, totally disregarding the existing human dynamics on the ground, ignoring the different tribes, languages, historical resources of locals, and longstanding tribal conflicts. In fact, the Europeans subsequently used these tribal conflicts to their advantage by pitting certain tribes against each other. In this way, local tribes would deliver enemy captors (future slaves) to Europeans for trade items, including guns.

This became an important tool in the colonialization process. One tribe favored by Europeans was put in power, while the others suffered. It is recorded that Europeans were so ruthless that after these "friendly" tribes brought captive slaves to them, when the native slave supply was depleted, they then made their own slave hunters their next slave victims. Invariably, we still have modern-day conflicts in Africa like the Tutsis and Hutus as the results of the wounds of this colonial separation process. So, Africa was cut up into various countries (50) at that time. This deliberate European carving up of Africa is a fundamental root cause of systematic disorder and upheaval of African society today. In addition to the many existing African languages and dialects, now the colonizers injected their own European languages (French, English, Portuguese, Dutch, German, etc.) and currencies into these newly formed countries, creating an even greater barrier to African unification of its countries and peoples.

Yet today, the world wonders why African countries have had difficulty thriving. Clearly, as we reflect on Chirac's earlier statement, Africa has experienced much turmoil since the introduction of European colonialism. Over hundreds of years, Africans have been attacked physically, mentally, and spiritually and *yet they survive*. In the Congo itself, it is recorded that King Leopold of Belgium (1835- 1909) killed and maimed over half of the population of the country (10 – 15 million) while extracting rubber, ivory, and other valuable resources. The Belgians even resorted to taking an allied African King's own family members as slaves to continue meeting quotas on valuable goods sent back to Belgium.

Every Black American family today is directly impacted by the European Atlantic Slave Trade, as our ancestors paid with their lives, culture, and dignity as they were enslaved for hundreds of years. This slave mentality produced a white supremist culture that setup a government that damaged black citizens at every turn to this day. However, it was not just Europeans in this brutal slave business. While we know Europeans ravaged western Africa, some may be surprised to learn that Arab nations had a similar history of taking slaves on the east coast of Africa. To be honest, the ruthlessness, and duration of the Arab *slave business* makes the Atlantic Slave Trade look mild in comparison. They killed and maimed over 75 to 100 million of our African ancestors over approximately 1000 years.

Blacks' Long, Rich History

The results of these events are that as Africans in America (Black citizens), we have been treated with utter disdain. We are told that we have no history—that we have no value. This has become a huge psychological anvil around some our necks, particularly for our young. Are we worthless? Did Europeans save us savages from the jungles, put clothes on our backs, feed us, and finally lead us to God? This is frankly the enduring tale that Europeans would have us believe. The truth is that Africa had many large thriving cities long before Europeans arrived on the scene. It is no surprise that African cultures crumbled as millions of its people were brutally killed and/or taken from their homelands.

This picture of "NO HISTORY" is a portrait skillfully painted by the European *slave master*, imposed through books, and well-thought-out educational schemes, popular movies, etc., as mechanisms for control. Until recently, it has been a masterpiece of deception. However, for decades now, learned Black scholars have been dismantling this narrative. The Black masses now are demanding the truth, our truth. However, we cannot depend on our former or even current oppressors to be our teachers or to reveal *our* truth in their telling of history. Even now, the white power structure is whole-heartedly denouncing the *1619 Project* in Congress *(which simply asks that TRUE history be taught in classrooms)*. White scholars' research and books have limited and twisted the truth to support their initial colonial goal, and continuing goal of white supremacy. It is to our benefit that we do our own search for truth. *KNOW-*

LEGDE IS POWER, which is precisely why whites have historically tried to keep Blacks as uneducated, second-class citizens and out of the power structure. Now there is a movement by some to keep black history totally out of public schools!

How will we as Black Americans learn the truth about our history in the American school system? A system that during the period of colonization was willing to kill Blacks for just learning to read, or cut off their limbs, or whip them mercilessly for having a book in their possession. For those in power, it was imperative that Blacks stay unschooled and uneducated—stupid! Largely, today's local school systems are a byproduct of European colonization. It is clearly apparent that a true complete telling of Black's citizen's history is being deliberately suppressed in the American classroom in favor of the narrow-cherry-picked **slave history.**

In 1933, Black scholar Carter G. Woodson (the 2nd Black Harvard Ph. D recipient) wrote his classic book *The Miseducation of the American Negro.* The basic message of the book is that Europeans (whites) enslaved and murdered millions of our Black ancestors, and then set up a system to not only control and dominate Blacks physically, but also most importantly to control us mentally through their educational system and their religion. Thus, we have been totally, purposefully *miseducated* by Europeans about our history. We are taught that anything of value, i.e., education, science, art, and religion, originated with them. Today, they continue to devalue and degrade Black intelligence. For the truth, we must study the works by other credible historians—*black American and African scholars.*

While there are some truthful European scholars, there are as many, or more, who have knowingly, or perhaps unknowingly, embraced the American and European racist educational systems. These systems are designed to continue the myth of Black people's non-history, backwardness, and inferiority, thereby perpetuating the *White Master Plan* for dominance over Blacks and other people of color.

Until the last five decades or so, the European narrative of *African savages* has even caused a significant percentage of Black Americans to be ashamed of Africa. To be honest, this is understandable because previously the Black masses had grown up in a system with an overwhelming constant barrage of negative images of Africans and Africa. We are taught to be purposely dismissive about these "shit hole" countries, as a former American President called them. Even a large percentage of uninformed Black Americans were cynical about Africans. How many of us have until recently had any real desire to visit our homeland but were very excited about visiting European countries— like France, Italy, or even Asian countries—that are constantly marketed to us through the media? I must admit, I have only recently visited Africa myself (2018). It was a truly rewarding experience to see our homeland. This adverse feeling toward Africa has been imposed and imprinted on our minds throughout our lives by the European influence of American books, television, and movies.

American society teaches, and solely promotes, the European narrative on life and history. Remember, *controlling the mind means you control the body*. When we were in grade school the American Education system taught that Columbus was a hero for discovering America (The New World), *as Columbus Day* was a national holiday! In fact, this indoctrination of lies starts very early in a child's educational process. I still remember as a young kid reciting, "*in 1492 Columbus sailed the ocean blue*." Today, history recognizes that Columbus did NOT discover America and that he was one of the primary people responsible for the *Atlantic Slave Trade*. He himself enthusiastically sent Native American slaves back to the Queen of Spain as gifts. In fact, in his book, "*They came before Columbus*," Black scholar, Dr. Ivan Van Sertima documents many written and visual accounts of the presence of Blacks in America long before Columbus. Van Sertima even appeared before the U.S. congress (1987) to present his findings to stunned, and yes, skeptical white lawmakers.

Yet Columbus' voyage was the precursor to the near total extermination of the Indigenous people of America at the hands of Europeans. Columbus called them Indians because he thought he had landed in India. He did not discover America; he had stumbled upon it. In his book "*Columbus and the Afrikan Holocaust*," Dr. John Henrik Clarke cites many of the atrocities by Columbus, and the resulting impacts on the lives of Native Americans and Black Africans. Much of Dr. Clark's information comes from Columbus' own ship logs of his expedition. Today that holiday, "Columbus Day," has been rebranded as "Indigenous Peoples Day." So, with knowledge (education) and the persistent demand for truth-telling, change is possible, even though it took 400 years.

Ancient Kemet (Egypt) and Africa

Black educators have found that Black history and the accomplishments of Black people are more truthfully told, and thus gain more credibility when written / documented and told by Black people. The people whose ancestors suffered the inhumane actions, those who claim Africa as their mother land. Therefore, those of us seeking to know the truth must seek sources beyond the biased early, and modern European scholars (some of whom had never set foot in Africa) to learn our history —this means we must seek to learn from *Black scholars*!

In African/Egyptian history, no one is more capable of telling the history of Black brilliance than the late **Dr. Cheikh Anta Diop** (1923–1986). Diop was a French-speaking African scholar from Senegal. In 1974, he set the European world on its heels by putting forth a detailed, researched thesis that Africa is the origin of world civilization. Diop graduated from Sorbonne University, the most prestigious university in France at time. He was a physicist, scientist, historian, linguist, and Egyptologist. Of all the Black scholars and academics on this subject, Diop was held in the highest esteem by black American and African scholars, although Europeans scholars still scoffed at the notion of any African importance in history. Black American scholars respectfully referred to Diop as the "Pharaoh." Diop has written many books on the Ancient Egyptians and their beginnings in the Nile Valley. Today, Cheikh Anta Diop University of Dakar, Senegal stands as his legacy.

His work was so controversial at the time that the European educational powers refused to accept the premise of his thesis. This push back by white power brokers meant that it took ten years for Diop to get his doctorate on the subject. Black Americans were late to learn of Diop and his *African Origin of world Civilization* argument because his early works were originally published only in French (almost ten years earlier) so he was not initially widely known. With the help of his American colleagues, like Dr. John Henrik Clarke, Diop's works were eventually translated into English and published in the United States in 1974. His most popular book, is *The African Origin of Civilization: Myth or Reality?* Black American historical thinkers bonded with Diop to launch a united process of discovery for Black Americans and their Black African brothers and sisters to reveal the truth of our being.

Diop's study found that the Ancient Egyptian language is rooted in African languages, being closest to Yoruba, and *Wolof,* his own native Senegalese language. He documents over 3,000 words in Egyptian Coptic and Wolof and their meanings to prove this. As a young chemist, Diop worked in the radio-carbon laboratory of renowned French scientist and Noble award winners for chemistry, Marie, and Pierre Curie. There he perfected a process to study skin cells to determine the melanin count in human skin, i.e., European versus Black Africans. This, he believed, could conclusively determine the skin color of mummies of early pharaohs. Melanin is a component that produces the dark hue in our skin. Unfortunately, antiquities authorities in Egypt would not provide skin samples from the most prominent older mummies needed to verify skin color. Still the visual appearances of these "black" mummified persons is undeniable.

Why is Egypt so important to African history? Diop believed that "**the history of Black Africans will remain suspended in air and cannot be written correctly until African Historians dare to connect it to the history of Egypt**." This he sought to do. His work was groundbreaking, and of course, as stated, European educators aggressively rejected his hypothesis. Yet today, the reality of an African Egypt has become more and more accepted by black and white scholars alike.

In 1974, Diop and his African colleague, Dr. Théophile Obenga, so convinced and empowered by the true story of Egypt, presented their findings at the UNESCO (United Nations Educational, Scientific and Cultural Organization) Conference in Cairo, Egypt. Attending the conference were 18 of the world's leading experts/thinkers on Ancient Egypt. An advanced invitation was given by UNESCO that asked these scholars to come prepared to discuss the origins of civilization. Diop and his colleague, Obenga, came well prepared and were able to make a strong case for their position and research that Africa is the origin of civilization, with Black Egypt as the cultural center of the Nile Valley. See Map-Exhibit B.

These two Black scholars based their argument on four distinct factors:

1. **Culture**: Egypt's culture can be proven to be rooted in African cultures.
2. **Language**: Egyptian language is closely related to the African language—Wolof of Senegal.
3. **Art**: Ancient paintings, sculptures, and monuments clearly depict Negroid/African figures.
4. **Historical Writings**: Ancient historians repeatedly referred to Egyptians as Black people.

These two brilliant Black professionals, presenting evidence along these four tracks, were able to expertly rebut any argument or rationale that Ancient Egypt was a European or Semitic civilization, to the degree that the opposing *experts* finally remarked, *"Well the Egyptian's color does NOT really matter, their accomplishments are what we are concerned with."* They knew they were being defeated and wanted to move away from the color issue. A narrative of this UNESCO conference by Professor Ivan Van Sertima is on YouTube—you must look at this; it is inspiring! Diop's and Obenga's research and conclusions were noted by UNESCO as being very thought provoking and well research and are printed in the UNESCO–Volume 2 of the series–The History of Africa. Language, one of the above key factors of Diop / Obenga's arguments at the Cairo Conference (1974) may be the most important and relevant factor in sorting out ancient people's place of origin, and culture, even more important than DNA.

Modern Historian, and Professor of Linguistics at UCLA, Dr. Christopher Ehret, in his Huggins Center symposium on YouTube "Africanity of Egypt" – 2019 speaks to this point. Professor Ehret states "while DNA/Genetics is considered a *fail proof* way of identifying people's origins/race it is subject to the sample sizes." Therefore, the mechanisms of the study, and truth-fulness of the study's authors can be manipulated. For example, to study DNA or fossil remains of an individual or set number of individuals during a certain period of history (Ancient Egypt) is NOT convincing scientific data, since this will speak *only* to that specific dataset (individual) or set of fossils and not the entire civilization. Any sample-set can rightly (or wrongly) be argued as valid, or invalid, as can be the appearance of art or monuments.

A much better way to reveal people's origin beyond Archaeology and DNA is **language and culture.** In this case Dr. Ehret utilizes language to expertly identify the Egyptians as being of African origins. Genes and DNA will reveal particular aspects of an ancient Egyptian person, but **language and culture** more correctly identify the origins of the "ancient peoples of Egypt" as a group – not based on color. He travels back deep in time and points to the proof of language groups in Africa. He identifies 2 primary language groups - both from 16,000 +/- years ago near the Horn of Africa

- Cushitic (Southern, East Africa, Horn of Africa)
- Omotic (East Africa)

A third - Afro Asiatic (not Semitic considered) later spread to North Africa. Yet, the two primary languages branched out and developed into still other languages. Words, language, is better at correctly identifying a group of people and their culture back through history than DNA. Dr. Ehret uses ancient Wild Grain as an example. It can be associated through art with the cycle shaped blade. This same art can be found in the LAGO OTA period of 16,000 BCE – Ethiopia, and the African culture of 15,000 BCE. Egypt was not a dry barren land at that time. They're existed great open plains where grain was the chief source of sustenance. Dr. Ehret points out that as wild grain began to be cultivated and harvested as a domestic crop around 6,000 BCE there became a cultural interchange and convergence of tribes in the Nile Valley, and Aswan / Nilo-Saharan, in the South of Egypt.

Dr. Ehret states that language spread as cultivation of crops spread from east and southern Africa leading to the numerous future African languages and dialects. Evidence shows that the Egyptian language originated from a Nilo-Saharan to Afro-Saharan family of languages from the south. As I mentioned earlier Diop listed over 1000 Egyptian words which are very similar to the Wolof language of Senegal (West Africa).

In terms of culture, there is no basis whatsoever for any argument that Ancient Egypt was rooted in European, Asian, or Semitic cultures, there is just no proof of this, no artifacts, or cultural connections to these countries. Beginning with the first Pharoah (from the south), Narmer Menes, all native Kings/Pharaohs came from the south. There is no such thing as "Black-White People!." There is not, nor has there ever been *indigenous "white tribes"* in Ancient Egypt, or Africa

These nagging stories of white tribes persist among some racist historical writings. "The Hamitic Philosophy" as it is called is based on Biblical references to Noah's son Ham (who the Bible states populated Egypt) This is another inference to supposed whites being responsible for Egypt in history. British explorer Henry Morton Stanley is reported to have run into these White Hamites on an expedition deep into Africa in 1869-1870. There is an interesting TEDx Talk on this subject of *The Hamitic Philosophy* by Micheal T. Robinson who specializes in the study of Historical Explorers and Expeditions. My first inclination was not to waste my time viewing this video - what I believed would be more false history. But I think it wise to hear alternate viewpoints to be better prepared to defend my own study. So, I clicked the *play* button. I was pleasantly surprised that Robinson totally obliterated this notion of *White Hamitic Tribes* in Africa. It was quite a serious presentation, but his conclusions were also humorous. Please check out his 2015 YouTube TEDx Talk video on the Hamitic Tribes – **and do watch to the very end!**

Black Scholars Reveal
Early Egyptians

Ancient Egypt was unknown to most Europeans. It was thought to be a barren, empty landscape over-run by the desert sand for over a thousand years. This perception was widely held until French General Napoleon Bonaparte, seeking other lands to conquer and bring under French domination, stumbled upon it during his conquest of Northern Africa. In 1798, he, in effect, rediscovered this ancient land for the masses. He thus opened a modern vast door to the glories and secrets of its past. This discovery triggered a frenzy of exploration by European archeologists and historians, along with the less noble treasure seekers, adventurers, and just plain criminals seeking to exploit the land and its riches.

One of Napoleons generals also found the renowned "Rosetta Stone," named for the city where it was found. This stone was critical in assisting modern man to finally be able to decipher "hieroglyphics" (what Egyptians called the Medu Netcher, or Holy Writings). This stone was created/written in 196 BC during the reign of Greek Pharaoh Ptolemy V. It contained one official government decree that was written in three languages inscribed on its face, namely Egyptian Demotic, Greek, and of course, the Hieroglyphics. Frenchman Jean-François Champollion (1790–1832) is largely given credit for deciphering the languages leading to the understanding of hieroglyph writings on temple walls, tombs, statues, and papyri throughout the Egyptian kingdom.

First, understand that the *real* name, the *original name* of Egypt for at least 3500 years, was **KMT** (*pronounced KEMET*). This is what the peoples of the land called it. When the Greeks conquered the land in 332 BC, they renamed it Egypt. However, for the entire rule of the Pharaonic Dynasties, the land was called Kemet, which means *Land of the Blacks*. This book should be properly called, *"Notes on Ancient Kemet,"* but I fear a large segment of the population would not be familiar with this name. Black Kushites, Nubians, Ethiopians, and other even more ancient branch tribes of Africans (such as the Anu) were the first inhabitants of the Nile Valley and Kemet.

As stated much of my information comes from reading the works of Black scholars, but also the testimonies of early European historians. As mentioned, 18th century Europeans in most cases knew the truth, but chose to distort the truth for their own selfish, oppressive purposes. Black scholars, our educators, are now anxious to tell us the truth about our past. The addition of Black/African Studies curriculum to many universities in the United States over the last four to five decades has been instrumental in correcting the centuries of lies about which Malcolm spoke. Also, there *are* many "truth-telling" ancient European scholars who reinforce Diop's views. These are most notably the ancient Greeks who wrote extensively, recorded, and documented their findings regarding Ancient Egypt.

In addition to Diop, African American scholars of note on this subject are as mentioned: Dr. John Henrik Clarke, Dr. Ivan Van Sertima, Dr. Chancellor Williams, Dr. Asa Hilliard, and Dr. Drusilla Dundee Houston, to name just a few. A more current scholar on Ancient Kemet is Egyptologist Anthony T. Browder. His books and videos are readily available today as part of his IKG.info.com site online, and on YouTube. I recently joined Browder's "Light of the World Egyptian Tour" in July of 2022.

The Nile River was, and still is, the life blood of Kemet. People of the early Nile Valley are known to have migrated down from the Great Rift Valley of East Africa's Ethiopia, Kenya, Somalia, Uganda, and Rwanda over 40,000 years ago. Ethiopians (meaning *burnt skin* in Greek) proudly proclaimed that the Egyptians were one of their colonies.

The very first Pharaoh of Egypt was named **Aha Narmer Menes** (Min) approximately 3200 BC: He united upper (Southern), and Lower (Northern) Egypt to form the world's first nation-state. Menes' rule was Dynasty 1 of 30 subsequent Dynasties and 3,200 years of this important advanced culture. Historical writings definitively state that he came from the South. Look at the attached map of Ancient Egypt (Exhibit B), or any map of Africa; it will show the countries south of Egypt are Nubia/Kush and Punt, modern-day Sudan, and Ethiopia. Down through history Europeans came to refer to all Black people as Ethiopians, because of the Greek *"burnt skin"* translation.

Dynastic Kemet lasted over 3,200 years, although pre-Dynastic civilization in the Nile Valley is believed to be 20,000 to 30,000 years older. These 30 Dynasties included over 300 pharaohs. A brief review of a few important names and places in Ancient Egypt follows Exhibit B.

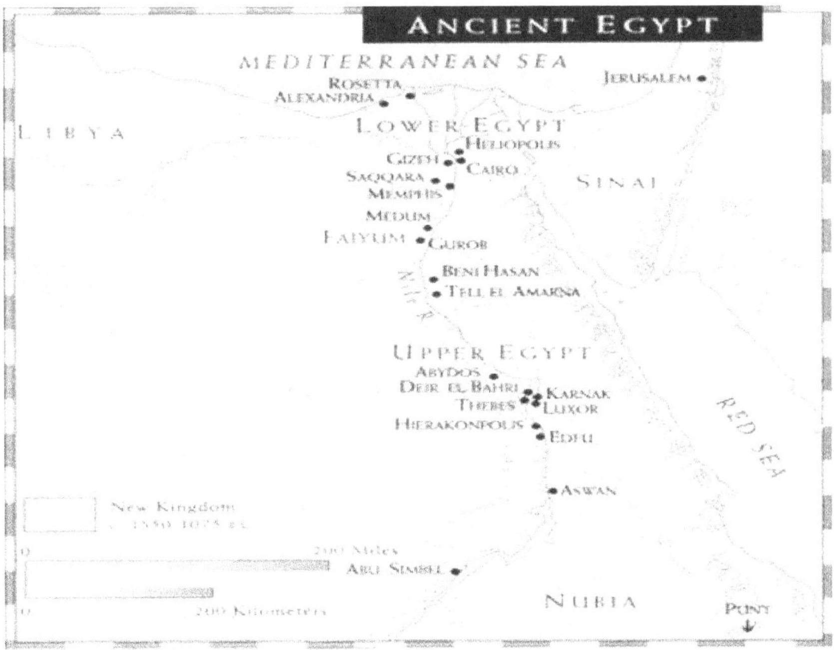

EXHIBIT B: MAP OF ANCIENT EGYPT

Imhotep is from the 3rd Dynasty 2650 BC. Although not a pharaoh, he was one of the most prominent figures in Egyptian history. He is considered by many to be the world's first known multi-genius. He designed and built the 1st

pyramid—the Stepped Pyramid at Saqqara in 2630 BC. The Pharaoh of this era was Djoser. Figures 2 & 4. *I'll mention more on Imhotep later.*

The Great Pyramid of Giza - Figure 5, 4th Dynasty–2589 BC. Over *2.5 million stones*, with an average weight of 2 tons each, make up the Pyramid, with some stones weighing up to 60 tons. This structure was an amazing 42 stories high. One account says that it took 20 years and 100,000 workers to build the Great Pyramid, <u>but to be clear, no one really knows</u>. It is still standing over 5,000 years later as one of the 10 wonders of the ancient world. The Pharaoh of this time was Khufu. This was the tallest structure on earth for over 4,000 years—designed and built by Africans.

Pharaoh Akhenaten - 18th Dynasty (1353–1326 BC). Akhenaten, originally named Amenhotep IV, was an important Pharaoh who initiated the "One God" worship (monotheism), was the Father of Tutankhamen, husband of Queen Nefertiti; and 10th Pharaoh of the 18th Dynasty. He also stated that there should be No Images made of GOD, this before the Biblical Moses. See Figure 7

Tutankhamen (1332–1323 BC) of the 18th dynasty was the boy king whose tomb was discovered in 1922 by Howard Carter. He ruled for about 10 years. He died approximately at 19 years of age. This tomb which contained the solid gold Death Mask continues to be the greatest trove of riches ever found in Egypt. Tutankhamen is verified by DNA to be Akhenaten's son – Figure 8

Rameses II (the Great) of the 19th Dynasty (1279–1213 BC) was the greatest Egyptian Builder and warrior, son of Seti I, husband of Queen Nefertari. He reigned in Egypt for sixty-seven years. Hollywood wrongly portrayed Rameses II as the Pharaoh of the Bible who ousted Moses and the Israelites from Egypt.

Cleopatra was the last Pharaoh of Egypt after 3,200 years of Dynastic Reign. Her reign marked the end of the Dynastic Period in 30 BC. She belonged to the 30th Dynasty. It is true that Egypt during Cleopatra's reign was on its last leg. The glory days were long past. So other than her being a female and the *last* pharaoh, her relationships with eventual Roman conquerors, Caesar, and Antony, are of note in history. This was a period of transition to Roman rule and historically significant. Her father, Ptolemy VII, was of course of Greek lineage, her sister, Arsinoe is believed to be of African heritage based on remains discovered in Turkey (where she fled for her safety), thought to be hers.

These remains were designated Nubian after DNA testing. Because of this; Cleopatra is also thought to be of an African mother.

Other well-known accomplishments attributed to Egyptians are The Sphinx, many spectacular temples, obelisks, astrology, art, math, medicine, philosophy, law, 24-hour days and 7-day weeks, and 365 ¼ day calendar year (4,000 years ago). The oldest known recorded date in human history is 4,260 BC—from the ancient Egyptian Calendar at Nabta Playa. See Figure 9, for additional information on the relevance of Nabta Playa. These and many more are all examples of the intellect, and genius of Black people. **I ask you to please pause here for a moment! As the young folks would say _marinate_ on this fact for a few moments: Europe, Greece and Rome did not even exist as countries until almost 2 thousand years after the pyramids were built!!**—approximately 800 BC for Greece, and 700 BC for Rome! They were the uncouth, savage, barbarians of the time. They get ZERO credit for impacting Egyptian culture and civilization.

Yet, in the Europeans' (white man's) view, there is _NO WAY_ that a Black people could have had anything to do with the above-named amazing accomplishments. They speak of Egypt as if it is its own separate island—NOT on the African continent. The truth is that thousands of years ago, the world's original people, Black people, migrated out of East Africa far and wide. There is hardly a country in the world today that has not been impacted by African peoples during their ancient existence. Although today globally all people with black skin have been marginalized by racism.

As stated, Kemet was a thriving civilization hundreds of years even before Pharoah Narmer Menes came to power. He did not create this civilization, but he did unify the upper and lower regions into one nation and helped to push it in the direction of legendary greatness. Thus, his name remains prominent in ancient world history. Two thousand years later, the Greeks named the land "Egypt." You will find that almost all terms and names we use today to refer to Egypt and its culture are, in fact, Greek words. For example, the Egyptian word for Pyramid is _Mir_, and _Tekhenu_ is the original name of the Obelisk. Once the Greeks conquered and took control of the land, they proceeded to change all names to their language for control and convenience. Anthony Browder feels it is important for blacks to recognize and embrace these true names of Kemet where possible.

The Nile River was the key to life in Kemet in ancient times. It was responsible for Kemet's success in farming, agriculture, and animal husbandry. The yearly flooding of the Nile produced rich topsoil perfect for planting crops and thus the success in feeding the nation. The flooding was a result of water coming down to (lower) Egypt from the *(upper)* inner highlands of East Africa, flowing south to north and ultimately into the Mediterranean Sea. As stated, Europeans have long claimed that Ancient Egypt was not inhabited by Blacks. They fervently hold to their cleverly crafted story that KMT meant *black land or black soil*, NOT *Black peoples*. This has been their argument, or "fake news" - printed in books and espoused during lectures for the last 200 years.

History clearly shows that ancient Black cultures existed exclusively in the Nile Valley. The Anu is one of the older known Black races of people probably from the same migration of peoples from Kush, Ethiopia and Somalia who inhabited Kemet in the early years before the unification of the two lands. These groups lived in the Nile Valley before spreading throughout northern Africa in hunter-gatherer, and later planting clans. In addition, Ta-Seti, meaning "Land of the Bow," (recognizing the skilled use of the bow by its warriors), was a Nubian society located in Quastul the capital city of Nubia. Ta -Seti is recorded as being some 200 years older than Kemet. **There, a *stone incense burner* was discovered with distinctive art on its face that is later seen on Egyptian temple walls, and monuments proving the direct connection of Black Africans to Ancient Egypt.**

Blacks existed long before Europeans appeared on earth. It is no stretch then to say Blacks ruled the world at that time. History clearly states that long before the founding of Kemet as a nation, Blacks had migrated throughout the *entire* Mediterranean region and beyond as shown by the testimonies below of noted European historians and scholars. Kemet, at its height, ruled over 100 hundred countries around the Mediterranean and the known world. See below.

A) Baldwin (Prehistoric Nations)—*Kushites/Ethiopians are older than Egypt; from 7,000 to 8,000 BC Cushite colonies resided in the Nile Valley. In 5,000 BC Egypt and Chaldea separate.*

B) Sir Godfrey Higgins—*There are two lands called Ethiopia—one east of the Red Sea, one west of the Red Sea, and another great nation of India to most of Asia.*

C) Huxley—*The Cushite Empire of Ethiopians ruled over three continents for thousands of years including the entire Mediterranean and Islands. Blacks ruled most of the known world.*

D) C.T. Volney - *Black tribes along the upper Nile were studying the stars 17,000 years ago.*

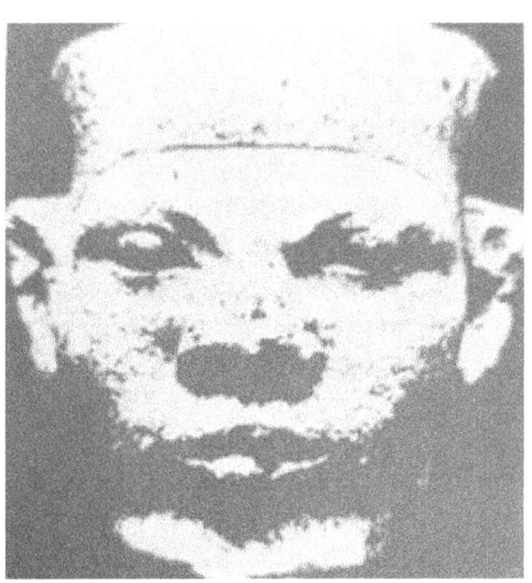

FIGURE1: NARMER MENES — EGYPT'S 1ST PHARAOH 3150 BCE

FIGURE 2 : IMHOTEP 3RD DYNASTY (2590 BCE)

FIGURE 3: PHARAOH KHUFU 4TH DYNASTY (2560 BCE)

FIGURE 4 : THE STEPPED PYRAMID AT SAQQARA MORTUARY COMPLEX – 3TH DYNASTY - 1ST EVER PYRAMID

FIGURE 5 : THE GREAT PYRAMIDS OF GIZA - 4TH DYNASTY 2580 BC

FIGURE 6: THE SPHINX – HEAD BELIEVED TO BE OF PHARAOH KHAFRE,
SON OF KHUFU

FIGURE 7 : PHARAOH AKHENATEN   FIGURE 8 : PHARAOH TUTANKAMEN

FIGURE 9: ANCIENT STONE CIRLCE CALENDAR

More on Nabta Playa: This immensely important and iconic Calendar is considered the world's first Astronomical Site (7,000 years old). This unique Stone Calendar was discovered at Nabta Playa in the barren, ancient Egyptian desert, 700 miles south of Cairo and 70 miles east of Aswan. *Initially it was thought to be random monoliths constructed by ancient peoples.* Modern Egyptologists, scientists, and astrological experts years later determined that the stone locations, and openings of the circle aligned with the moon and stars at particular times each year, marking the start or change in seasons - summer, spring, and fall - in affect a "circular calendar".

This understanding of the seasons (knowing when the inundation would come each year) was critical to Egypt's success as a nation in feeding its people. Ancient Egyptians priest studied the stars for perhaps 17,000 years ago. They placed great importance on the cycles of the sun, moon and stars. In fact most temples and monuments are proven to be built along orientations of heavenly bodies in the night sky. Nabta Playa was discovered in 1973, but critical understanding of the *Circle* was not accomplished until 1998. Today the calendar stands on the site of the Nubian Museum in Aswan. The book *Black Genesis* by Robert Bauval & Thomas Brophy goes into great astronomical detail in explaining Nabta Playa, and the "Ancient Calendar".

First Humans—Black

Scientists agree that Blacks were the "first of all peoples" (homo sapiens sapiens) on earth, originating in Africa. It stands to reason then that the first humans to reach Europe over 40,000 years ago were also Black Africans (Grimaldi Negro skeletons) as verified by the discovery of skulls found in the Mousterian Period in Italy. This is the period in which the last Neanderthals lived.

As stated earlier, there is NO scientific evidence of other Homo Sapiens-Sapiens that precede the Grimaldi Man in Europe or Asia. Neanderthals are Hominins, Homo Sapiens, but NOT Homo Sapiens-Sapiens. They are designated as cousins, not brothers of Homo-Sapiens-Sapiens. Denisovans have now replaced Cro-Magnons as a species by scientists. The Neanderthals species are believed to be last in Europe 40,000 to 80,000 years ago; Cro-Magnon (Denisovans) species were in Spain 20,000 years ago. All these species are now extinct. These are the last signs of what we called the *caveman*. Denisovans are a relatively newly discovered ancestor of eastern Europe/Asia.

Modern scientists explain that these people, early European homo sapiens, were caught in the Ice Age (a Glaciation Period) in Europe. The weather was so brutally cold that they had to take refuge in caves for survival. This ice event lasted 20,000 years and ended 12,000 years ago. During this Ice Age, those original people who left Africa (represented by Grimaldi negro) over thousands of years ago, were transformed through natural adaptation. It is believed they evolved to develop white skin because of extremely harsh, cold, darkness. This resulted in the loss of "melanin" (the critical molecule which produces skin colorization). The loss of melanin along with certain gene mutations, like albinism (albino people) are contributors to the subsequent appearance of pale colorless skin of the Europeans. A less impactful, but similar occurrence can be pointed to for context. This is when the Brown Bear from Ireland migrated North (40,000 to 50,000 years ago) into a similar harsh environment. Through natural selection and adaptation, this species, over a long period, became the white Polar Bear.

In like fashion, the Cro-Magnon/Denisovans are believed to be a mutation of the Grimaldi Negroid Man due to existing 20,000 years in an extreme harsh, cold environment. The Denisovans later interbred with the Neanderthals in this cold environment. Over thousands of years, eventually the first modern European (white man) appeared. This interbreeding is why virtually all Europeans have a small percentage of Neanderthal genes, 1-2% in their DNA.

To be direct, please understand that today's white race of Europeans is a mutation (not evolution), of the original Black human. Look it up; the evidence is there. In fact, ALL other peoples on earth are derived from that original migration of Black peoples out of Africa. Different climatic impacts, subsequent interbreeding, and other gene and environmental factors produced the different colors of peoples today over thousands of years, but the *anatomical bone structure is unchanged from the 1ˢᵗ Black Homo sapiens-sapiens*. Only skin color, hair texture, eye color, and other gene features have changed, and we know that skin color and hair texture, etc., are NOT physical determinates of Homo-sapiens-sapiens designation; *only the bone structure and genetics/DNA are key*. Because of this, the white man should NOT be at the end of that human development chain spoken of earlier. For emphasis, all peoples today have the same basic anatomical structure as the first Black Homo sapiens-sapiens thousands of years ago! White skin is not an *evolutionary* identifier of Homo sapiens-sapiens. There is only one race of people - humans!

A curious situation that must be dealt with here is the existence of black populations with straight hair, and some with blue eyes. Are these Africans, "white people" with black skin, or some other designation? The Dravidians of India, for example, are an extremely dark, very large population of black people with straight hair. The island of Melanesia is a place where many blacks have blond hair. The unique appearance of these people is, perhaps, how Europeans tried to validate their claim of "black - white people," therefore characterizing black Egyptians as being white. Africans, as previously stated come in all sizes, colors, and facial traits. These Dravidian people still are a people originating in Africa, even with straight hair. Diop indicates there were two black races with different characteristics: one with wooly hair and fleshy noses; the other likewise has black skin (*often exceptionally black)*, with straight hair, thin lips, and narrow noses. We can identify a segment of Nubians with these same traits. Diop pointed to the words of an early Arab writer, Edrissi, who stated that, " *Nubians are the most handsome of blacks; their women have thin lips and straight hair.*" So, the Dravidian is likely closely related to this same segment of Nubian peoples who obviously migrated out of Africa in ancient times into India and neighboring countries. Today, it is still possible to find some black Africans with wooly hair and blue eyes; these gene variations are indeed still prevalent.

Dr. Nina Jablonski is a professor of Anthropology and Paleoanthropology at the University of Pennsylvania. She is a prominent scholar of skin pigmentation and the origin of skin color. She writes extensively about melanin, dark skin versus white skin. Her data and research explain the scientific reason why the original humans by necessity had to have dark skin pigmentation. These humans basically HAD to have lots of melanin in their skin, or they would not have survived the intense heat of the region at the equator where they originated. The determining factors have to do with the extreme amounts of ultraviolet rays (UVR) generated by the sun at the equator in Sudan, Kenya, Ethiopia, etc. The melanin, and the amount of vitamin D was, and still is, critical to human survival in that region. Melanin is extremely important to the function of the entire body.

Scientists believe that over thousands of years our furry hominin relatives began to shed their fur/hair. Those in Africa near the equator, a severely hot climate, adapted by developing a more melanin-filled skin, darker skin, to protect them from the blazing sun and damaging effects of UV rays. Their bodies produced sweat glands to regulate heat to cool them down. You will notice that animals with fur, have great difficulty in cooling down, panting profusely, always seeking mid-day shade. This new upright man, Homo Sapiens Sapiens, had to travel great distances in the sun in search of food and shelter, releasing body heat was critical to survival, thus no fur.

Professor Jablonski points out that once our ancient relatives (Homo Sapiens Sapiens) migrated out of Africa northward into Europe, the severe colder weather of the glaciation period and less danger from UV rays resulted in a slow, natural environmental process that resulted in a loss of melanin, *thus, a loss in skin pigmentation over thousands of years occurred.* Her research shows that these people made up for the lack of vitamin D from the sun by eating foods rich in vitamin D like grains and fish. Also, recessive gene factors, and gene mutations in DNA are contributors to the loss of skin color. Remember that albinism, (or Albinos) also is the result of certain recessive gene impacts. These factors are how white people (Europeans) came to be. Black people were on earth long before mutated whites appeared. Professor Jablonski has written many books on this subject, and her lectures can be found on YouTube (Evolution and Meaning of Human Skin Color – 2020). Her data is cogent, credible, and simply fascinating. Every person, Black or white, should be knowledgeable about this data, the whitening or depigmentation process of the skin.

After this severe climate event ended, these transformed Black people of Europe started to emerge from the dark, cold environment of Europe —now white in skin color. They eventually began to interbreed with other species of hominins, including Neanderthals, Denisovans etc. producing modern European (white) with depigmentation of the skin over thousands of years. The Nile Valley appears to have been solely inhabited by Blacks from the origins of humanity up to the appearance of other races (now transformed races). Whites did not venture out of this ice age until 12,000 years ago. Just as Malcolm stated, Blacks lived in cities while Europeans still lived in caves. Therefore, it is *no surprise* that today this people, who were conditioned in cold weather, including those who later moved south, into historically hot climates, are highly susceptible to skin diseases and cancer caused by overexposure to high levels of UV rays. They are NOT made for these typically hot climates; it is simply the laws of nature at work.

Until the ending of this thousands of years "ice event" and subsequent migration of transformed people, there was no *documented mention* in history of a white race of people as a group appearing in Africa or Egypt. This was the situation, and it remained that way until historians spoke of an invading people into Egypt in 1730 BC. **The Hyksos, a Semitic/Asiatic people from**

eastern Europe, are the first foreign peoples documented to have entered Kemet as a large group. This invasion was during the XVII Dynasty. The Hyksos eventually conquered Northern Egypt and ruled for 150 to 200 years. These new rulers made the Egyptians slaves during their time in power and sparked one of Egypt's periods of social and political turmoil. There is some indication that the Hyksos were distant relatives of the Jews and is thought to be the reason why Jews were later treated badly by Egyptians in Ancient times according to the Bible. After their approximately 200-year reign in northern Egypt, Africans from the south, Nubians (King Ahmose-1550 BC) came north and defeated the Hyksos to restore Black control, and culture of Egypt in its entirety. Thus, there were admittedly non-Black pharaohs for what are called *Intermediate periods* in Egypt's history. Some scholars believe that the Biblical Joseph rose to power so fast in Egypt because he was a Semite, and the current pharaoh, and power structure of the time, were also Semites because of the Hyksos' control. After this time, there were many recorded invasions from other outside nations, thus producing other non-native Egyptian/African Pharaohs.

Greek Historians Validate
Egyptians As Black

Numerous Ancient Greek scholars over their time and travels in Egypt confirm that Ancient Egyptians were Black Africans. Chiefly among them was Herodotus.

Herodotus 480–425 BC (Father of History): *As for me, I judge the Colchians to be a colony of the Egyptians because, like them, they are Black and have wooly hair.*

Herodotus: *The uniform voice of primitive antiquity spoke of the Ethiopians as one single people, dwelling along the shores of the Southern Ocean from India to the Pillars of Hercules.*

Note: Herodotus is widely called the "Father of History" by European scholars because of his writings and extensive travel in Egypt, and other lands in the then known world during his lifetime. Yet, when he calls Egyptians a Black race, then his credibility is questioned by the same European (white) scholars who named him the "Father of History." Still, there are many, many similar statements by other scholars that identify the Egyptians as a Black people.

Race and discrimination were not big factors in ancient times, or in the period of classical Greco/Roman prominence. Black/Brown people were a part of all facets of life. Blacks were noblemen, politicians, soldiers, priests, artists, tradesmen, etc. Blacks were also, typically known as fierce soldiers – and fought in various armies. Even in Japan, it is recorded that to be a good Samurai, you need a "bit of black blood in your veins." We also have proof of three Black/Brown Popes, and African Roman Emperors as well. Though Romans and Greeks *did* refer to other races as *barbarians*, or *pagans*, it was not based on skin color, but on religious affiliation, or lack thereof. Yet, the issue of Black discrimination began to get a foothold in Egypt itself under Roman rule.

Blacks were noted only by the Greeks for the fact that they came from a place where the sun had burned their skin. Likewise, people with pale skin, blond hair and blue eyes were identified by Greeks as coming from places where cold and snow prevailed. One indication of the absence of a skin color bias, was the popular and well-accepted Shakespearian play, "Othello," which was written in 1603. This popular, well-known play was about the relationship a of Moor nobleman, Othello. Moors of the time were known to be Black, and he was constantly referred to as *the Moor*. His lover was a Venetian/European woman, Desdemona. The play was not centered on race, but rather it was about jealousy and betrayal. The play triggered no racial outrage as Blacks were everywhere, as typical members of society!

In early Europe and America, terms like swarthy, tawny, dusty and brunette were used to identify the complexion of black/brown people. The website "Newspaper Archives" reveal numerous articles in 1700 – 1900s of prominent peoples with this "brunette" complexion. Webster's dictionary of 1828 clearly refers to many prominent historical figures as tawny, swarthy and brunette as having brown skin color. Not until the early 20th century did *brunette* become a term used solely for hair color thanks to the rise of white supremacy. This was clear in newspaper articles, where individuals were described as having black hair, blue eyes *and then – with brunette or tawny skin complexions*. Modern day power elites have washed away these descriptive terms seeking to whiten history.

As shown earlier, the ancient Greeks' testimony made it clear that the Egyptians were a Black people, so when did this narrative change? It is documented that *approximately 1830 CE or so, is the period when modern European scholars began to deny the Black role in Egypt, and in history in general.* This denial corresponds with the rise of 18th and 19th century **European Imperialism**

(White Supremacy) and reinforced the tolerance and continued importance of Black slavery across the world. Also, for religious readers, understand that slavery was accepted, and even sanctioned by the Queen of England, the Pope, and the Christian Church, and Islam! Therefore, this allowed Christian and Islamic enslavers free reign to dominate and dehumanize an entire race of people — *as pagans and infidels*, as the religious zealots would identify them. I remind you, one of the very first slave ships to arrive in America was named "The Jesus."

French historian, Hegel, made Blacks sub-human when he wrote, ***"The negro is completely wild and untamed and is not part of the world. Africa has no history because Africans are not sufficiently human."*** Many American politicians felt the same way as Hegel. Thus, they enacted laws to constrict blacks' advancement, and rights as people. Europeans in America and other countries even went so far as to put some African people in zoos as viewing spectacles for white audiences. Such stereotypes have filled book after European book over hundreds of years! Europe was already deeply dedicated to the slave trade since the 1600s, so it fully promoted this belief of *nonhuman*, to justify African Slavery. Before 1830, Egypt was widely accepted as an African civilization, and was the source of Europe's own civilizing process by way of Greece. After 1830, there was a concerted, and successful effort by racist European academics to totally remove Blacks from Egypt, and Egypt from Africa.

Europeans (whites) set out to make "Black/Africans" ugly and worthless throughout the world. I dare say they were extremely successful in implementing their *master plan*. It is rare in 2022 for a current white teacher, scholar, or any modern-day Egyptian official (who are Arabs) to publicly acknowledge that Ancient Egyptians were Black Africans. The educational curriculum at the primary and/or high school level is NOT designed to teach the richness of ancient Black societies like the Nile Valley at all, but rather they readily identify Blacks and other native peoples in history books and videos as *savages*, or plain backward, to reinforce their sub-human rhetoric and propaganda. The singular focus on American/European history in schools sets the stage for the distinctive divide in humanity, supporting a divide between white students, and students of color. Teachers, some just following the curriculum, others unapologetic racists, are empowered to present films or photos of Indigenous people's nakedness, to the laughs and snickering of the young kids—Blacks and Whites alike in the classrooms, with no context or alternate discourse.

Today the current inhabitants of Egypt are Arabs. They would have you believe that their ancestors were the ancient civilization of pharaohs. But we know that Arabs did not invade and conquer Egypt until **654 CE** or over 2,000 years after the Great Pyramids and other temples and monuments were built (please look this up). As Dr. Ivan Van Sertima would proclaim, "They did not have a DAMN thing to do with the accomplishments of Ancient Egypt."

Again, more solid historical proof of the Black presence in Egypt can be had by studying the works of ancient writers, Greeks, and others. A few statements by ancient scholars are listed below.

Herodotus (480–425 BC), a Greek historian, is considered the "Father of History" by Europeans. He traveled extensively in Egypt. *He stated that a Greek oracle was known to be from Egypt because she was Black - "The natives of that region are Black with heat."*

Gaston Maspero (1846–1916), Italian historian: *"By almost unanimous testimony Egypt belonged to a negro race first settled in Ethiopia."*

Georg (German): *"Worldwide domination of Ethiopians, a Black race."*

Diodorus (50 BC), Italian historian: *"Ethiopians are the first of all men— They Colonized Egypt."*

Puranas—India Sanskrit texts: *"Ethiopian kings were worshiped in **India**. Dravidians lived from India to Spain."*

Gerald Massey, (British Author): *"The Egyptian book of Dead is the oldest religious writing known to man. Resurrection is first mentioned in Egyptian writings. Asar/Osiris was resurrected."*

James Brunson: *"Cushite Colonies all along the southern shores of Asia Minor."*

Wilford: *"Ethiopians openly mentioned in India Sanskrit writings."*

Heerden (Ancient Nations of Africa): *"Ancient ancestors of Ethiopians/Nubians had long resided in cities. Built magnificent structures, had laws and government. When Greeks scarcely knew Sicily by name, Ethiopians were celebrated in verses and poems."*

There exists an actual artist *rendering / painting inside the **Tomb of Pharoah Rameses III at Abydos (1200 BC)***. It is called the Book of Gates or the *Table* _of Nations_ (please, search the Internet for Table of Nations). It clearly shows how the Egyptians saw themselves—as Blacks!—and how they painted themselves at that time. This makes a clear distinction between the appearances (skin colors) and dress of Egyptians and Africans as Blacks, as compared to the Indo-European, and the Semite people who are depicted with lots of facial hair/ beards as non-blacks. This should end the controversy of skin color of the Ancient Egyptians—but sadly, it will not.

In addition, another solid statement of Egyptians color is the description and paintings used for the God Osiris (Greek for Ausar). It is well documented in Egyptian history that the pre-Dynastic God Osiris—the greatest of all Gods—is called the _"Lord of the Perfect Black" in the Egyptian Book of the Dead._

Finally, further validation of an African Egypt is a very solid one. When you look at African culture - _the practice of circumcision was distinctly African._ This practice is known to have originated in East Africa. History shows that Egyptian mummies as old as 4,000 BCE were circumcised. Herodotus stated that, _"alone among mankind, Ethiopians and Egyptians have practiced circumcision from time immemorial."_ This, because they shared the same African heritage.

Wallis Budge a leading 19th century historian, in his book _Egypt_ had this to say, _"The prehistoric native of Egypt, both in the old and new stones ages was African, and there is every reason for saying that the earliest settlers came from the south. There are many things in the manners, customs and religion of the historic Egyptians that suggest that the original home of their prehistoric ancestors was in a country in the neighborhood of Uganda and Punt."_

Dating Kemet (Egypt), The Bible, Jews/Hebrews

I repeat, the current inhabitants of Egypt are Arabs. Before they invaded Egypt, history clearly shows them to be desert nomads (Bedouins). There is no evidence in their early history or culture or large-scale building, agriculture, or civilization on their part. They are NOT the Egyptians of the Dynastic period. Again, they did not invade Egypt until 654 CE—long, long AFTER the time of the pharaohs. These Arabs, and now mixed-race peoples, have no connection to Ancient Egypt. They are the last of the many conquering nations of Egypt, over 600 years after the death of Cleopatra and the end of the Dynastic period.

In the information that follows, I will outline a few dates and timelines of conquering nations, pharaohs, and noteworthy events. They may seem extreme, so let me give a quick explanation of how the dates come about. The dates are derived by various methods, from Egyptian writings on Ancient Egyptian monuments and papyrus, to the writings by Greeks and other ancient peoples, and finally by modern scientific dating methods.

On the scientific side, one method of dating is called *Radiocarbon Dating*. A quick explanation: all living things are made of organic material, which are carbon based. They contain carbon 12 and 14. Carbon 14 is unstable and decays at consistent rate. The amount of carbon 14 in a sample is measured and compared to an internationally approved standard - look it up. This method generally entails sampling data of the layers in the earth's strata where excavations reveal bone fossils, and related volcanic ash, gravel, plants, tools, pottery, etc. One of the most recent dating methods today is called Potassium–Argon Dating. This method is believed to be accurate to billions of years. Lucy was dated using the Potassium–Argon method. Much like carbon dating, Potassium 40 decays at a consistent rate and generates Argon gas. Again, an approved International Measuring standard is utilized to approximate the amount of decay, resulting in the eventual calculating of dates. Dating of these fossils is extremely difficult/critical. It is a true science unto itself. They seek to date the bones of animals and humans - teeth, volcanic ash, plants, and other physical testing including DNA of fossils in specific areas. To fully grasp these methods of dating, I would suggest that the reader consider additional study of dating methods.

What role does religion play? Understand that religion is of extreme importance in human existence. It is a primary staple in the human experience. Most humans believe in a higher being. Early history indicates that even before there was such a thing as Kings or Queens, the power of clans, tribes and communities was predominately in the hands of spiritual leaders, witch doctors, shamans, or priests. They would control and mitigate spiritual matters plus daily life decisions of village/community direction. Religion still controls the lives and minds of millions upon millions of people today. As the first nation state in history, Egyptians had an extremely sound spiritual base as can be attested to by thousands of documented writings on papyrus, temple walls and monuments, and their reverence for their Gods. It is estimated that over 80,000 priests, artisans, administrators, etc., worked at the famed Karnack Temple in Luxor at the height of its existence. The Virgin Birth, One God, Resurrection, Hell/Hades, circumcision, the Ten Commandments (*Based on Egypt's 42 Negative Pronouncements of MAAT*) and more are all documented Ancient Egyptian spiritual ideas. Spirituality and worship were in place long before the establishment of Egypt as a nation, at least 4000 to 5000 BC. The Egyptian "Book of the Dead" and the earlier "Pyramid Text" are called the oldest spiritual writings in history dating back to 2400 BC. These *Funerary Texts*, consisting of what is called a series of "spells and mysteries," are meant to help the dead person rise (resurrected) and maneuver his/her way through to the spirit world – called a period of *transition*.

So, when and under what circumstances did we get the Bible? Records show that the bible was written over a period of approximately 1,500 years by up to 40 different people. **Is the Bible inspired by GOD?** Every religious person would say YES! But most scholars and historians have serious problems with the validity of Bible stories, people, and timelines. The Bible itself tells us that at creation "a day equated to or is like 1,000 years." It says that God created the world in 6 days, and on the 7th day he rested. Religious scholars believe a period *before time—"In the beginning was the WORD." Then sometime before 4000 BC was the CREATION.* So right away we can see that there is no correlation whatsoever between documented history and the Bible timeline. Science, written history, and the Bible are thousands of years apart in timelines.

Historical records show that Egypt had developed the world's first calendar by 4260 BC (this process of studying the stars took hundreds, if not thousands, of years in which to formulate a accurate modern calendar—365 ¼ days). If this is true, man was around long before the suggested Biblical 4000 BC creation date, or even 6000 BC. Biblical scholars and history books state that Hebrews (Jews) did not enter Egypt until about 1674 BC. By this time, the world-renown pyramids were already built and were over 1,000 years old! In addition, the spiritual concepts mentioned above were at least 1,000 years old before the Hebrews came to Egypt. So, the pyramids were NOT built by Hebrew (Jewish) slaves as depicted in Hollywood movies and popular stories. According to the Bible, Joseph, initially a slave, eventually brought his entire family into Egypt. Again, according to the Bible, Abraham, and his family—70 Hebrews (12 family groups)—entered Egypt in 1674 BC. The two Egyptian spiritual writings were very old by this time.

It can also be verified that a significant number of passages, statements and events of the biblical writings are very similar, if not identical to Egyptian writings and texts on monuments, papyrus, and spiritual writings produced over 1,000 years *before* the Bible, including the creator being called "the WORD." It is apparent that writers of the Bible borrowed extensively, and were greatly influenced by Ancient Egyptian religion, writings, and beliefs.

There are different versions on when the Biblical Israelites left Egypt, chased out by Pharaoh's army based on various Bible verses/calculations. This would basically determine who the pharaoh was at the time. Were Jews in Egypt for 430 years or 215 years? One scholar says the original Bible verse says the Jews were in *Canaan **and** Egypt* for 430 years. He used his calculation to say that they were in Egypt itself for only 215 years. If you subtract each one (430 or 215) from 1674 BC, you will arrive at different dates. Whichever one you accept, 1459 BC or 1244 BC, or some other date, would help in revealing who the Pharoah of the Exodus was. At any rate, no matter the date, one million (more or less) Jews including men, women and children are believed to have left Egypt, led by Moses. Bible scholars state that 1446 BC begins the Exodus from Egypt, so the date 1459 BC is at least in the same general timeline.

While the Egyptian tomb writings, the *Book of the Dead*, and many others, were written in real time, the Bible was written hundreds/thousands of years *after* the events it chronicles. The Israelites/Jews of the day were, basically, shepherds, and uneducated. When Moses, a man educated in Egypt, a former Egyptian official, first appeared with the 10 Commandments, very few people, at that time, if any, could read or write. Moses' exact birth date is still up for discussion, but some believe he lived during or after the reign of 18th Dynasty Pharaoh, Akhenaten (1358–1322 BC). Akhenaten was a key figure in Egyptian history. Remember he is the pharaoh who installed monotheism —ONE GOD worship in Egypt.

Akhenaten's reign and worship of the Sun God, Aten, put Egypt into great transition and upheaval since the existing priesthood, and political power structure objected vehemently to this change. As a result, Akhenaten and his followers moved south and built the city of Amarna. The Bible states that as a priest in Egypt, Moses was learned in all things Egyptian. Some believe that Moses learned the "One GOD" practice during his time in Egypt. So how did today's Bible come to be? How did it really come together? The Council of Nicaea (325 CE) will shed some light on this.

The City of Nicaea is where Emperor Constantine of Rome called together over 300 of his Bishops from around his empire and requisitioned the creation of ONE Bible, essentially one line of thought and belief system. He felt this new Bible would make it much easier to rule his vast empire because it had grown so large and had become too difficult to control its various factions. Here at this conference, the final Bible was crafted by these Bishops. They deleted some books and added others, ultimately making it more broadly acceptable to the empire, thus creating a means for the King to unite his people under the same spiritual line of thought. It is also here that these Bishops decided that December 25 would be designated Christ's birthday. So, the question remains, is the Bible inspired by God? Or did political considerations have a major impact in crafting this, Bible. Sorting out these biblical and historical stories can be a daunting task while trying to rectify teachings with historical and scientific study. Was the Bible written by the elites of the day under direction of the political power structure, or by God's spirit?

The popular King James version of the Bible is also said to have come into being for political reasons. Italy (Rome) and England were sometimes enemies, but historically always keen competitors. King James I of England did not want his subjects or his empire tied so inextricably to Rome by the Bible, even though both purported to be Christian nations. As a result, he requisitioned the King James version of the Bible to suit his Kingdom and his rule in 1611 CE. Again, this is history; please do your research on the origin of both important versions of the Bible. A large percentage of people around the world place the utmost importance in following these texts each day of their lives, trying to adhere to these "holy inspired writings."

A few Historical as well as Biblical "timelines" follow for your perusal.

NOTABLE TIMELINE INFORMATION AND CHRONOLOGY:

3168 – 2890 BC—*Narmer Menes (MIN) becomes 1ˢᵗ Pharaoh & King – 1ˢᵗ Dynasty of Egypt*

2650–2575 BC—*3ʳᵈ Dynasty—Pharaoh Djoser, Imhotep, built Stepped Pyramid*

2589–2566 BC—4ᵗʰ Dynasty *Khufu (Cheops) Pharaoh that built the Great Pyramid of Gisa*

1674 BC—First known record of Jews in Egypt

18ᵗʰ Dynasty—Called Egypt's the Golden Age—(1560–1294 BC) *Akhenaten, Tutankhamen, Hatshepsut, Rameses the Great—Temple @ Abu Simbel*

780 BC—25ᵗʰ Dynasty, *Kushite pharaohs ruled for 100 years—Shabaka, Pianki &Taharka are the most notable pharaohs. The XXV Dynasty marked the* **End of Black reign over Egypt.**

670 BC – Assyrians invade and conquer Egypt.

650 BC – 26ᵀᴴ Dynasty – The Saite Dynasty - Last Egyptian rule

525 BC—Persians Conquered Egypt

332 BC—Greeks Conquered Egypt—*Ptolemy 1 (Ptolemy, a General of Alexander the Great) became the 1ˢᵗ Greek Pharaoh; his family ruled for 300 years. Ptolemy VII was Cleopatra's father.*

50 BC—Romans conquered Egypt, *took control from Greeks—Julius Cesar, Marc Antony*

30 BC—*Cleopatra Queen of Egypt (her mother possibly a consort of African descent). Her father was Ptolemy VII, a Greek*

<u>000 CE—Birth of Jesus</u>

40 CE—*Apostle Paul brought Christianity to Egypt*

325 CE—Christian Bible, by decree of Emperor Constantine, Council of Nicaea 325 CE

330 CE—*Christianity accepted by Roman Emperor Constantine himself.*

570 CE—*Birth of Prophet Muhammed— birth of Islam*

645 CE—*Arab (Muslim) conquest of Egypt*

1798 CE—*Europeans, Napoleon (French) stumbled upon Egypt. This discovery would lead to the conquering and looting of the country. As stated, one of his generals also found The Rosetta Stone. This Stone had writings in hieroglyphics, Greek, and Demotic (Egyptian language). This is how scholars (Frenchman-Champollion) learned to decipher and translate hieroglyphics.*

See Exhibit C: Visual Historical Timeline

Visual Historical Timeline

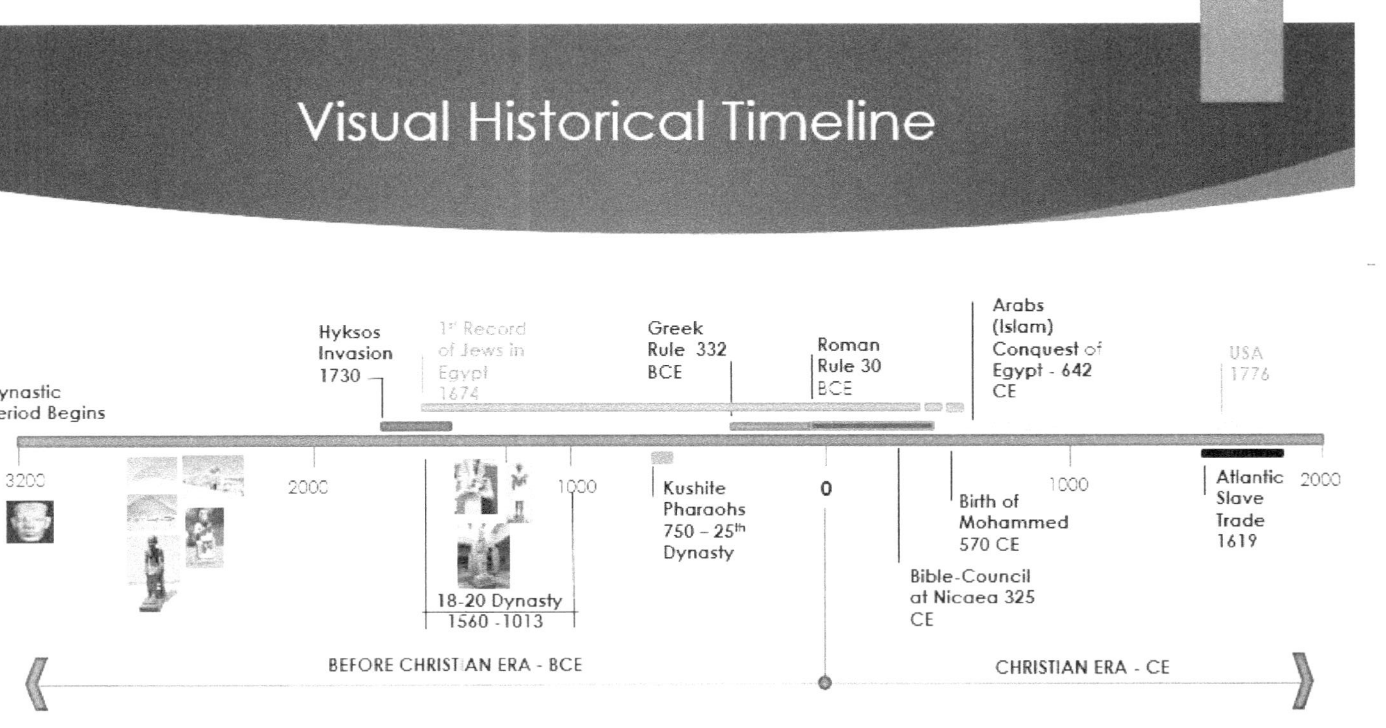

Exhibit C

Slavery In History

Slavery is a uniquely old institution. Who knows when it really began? What do we know about slavery in ancient times? Well, we know that there was NO color distinction for any people who were slaves, Blacks, Whites, Semites, etc.,—any peoples at some point could have, and did fall into this servitude by other marauding peoples. Most people at some time owned slaves themselves, even Africans! Remember the Bible tells us that even Joseph was a slave for some period in Egypt; this is because his brothers sold him into slavery to traveling merchants. History clearly shows that Europeans enslaved Europeans, just as Africans enslaved Africans. Europeans are quick to point out examples of *Africans killing Africans, to lessen the impact, or absolve themselves, of their killing of Africans.* But isn't the holocaust, and other known genocides such as Bosnia and Herzegovina, examples of Europeans massacring Europeans? Look now at Russian and Ukraine, no people are blameless in this regard.

History indicates the primary cause of people in slavery in ancient times was *captives of war*. Yet, financial reasons were also a typical cause for enslavement. Poor people sold themselves to pay off debts or sold their children for money as servants, etc. But slavery was not racial, and not necessarily a permanent status. You could pay off your debt and free yourself, or perhaps your time as a slave was fulfilled. There is also documentation of freed, or runaway slaves in history becoming rich themselves. So many forms of slavery have been around for thousands of years no matter what your skin color.

Dr. John Henrik Clarke states, "Without diminishing the German/European Jewish Holocaust resulting in the death of 6 million Jews, the *African Holocaust was the greatest single crime in world history committed against a people.*" The estimated death toll of Africans, he states, "*Begins at 60 million. . .Nothing else on earth can match this massive genocide and destruction.*" It is believed that 10 million Africans were taken from Africa to North Americas, and another 20 to 40 million were taken to South America. To add insult to injury, it is estimated that millions of more Africans on the continent were killed or died as result of this European "business plan." Dr. Clarke also calls this *slave trade* a *designed economic movement* that revealed the "first glimpses of *European-type Capitalism.*" These atrocities against humanity in the "new world" was started by Columbus. The journals of his voyages also reveal that he sent Indigenous peoples as slaves back to the Queen as gifts.

In the *New World (America)*, initially European colonists sought to use Europeans slaves, as they had already been doing so in their homeland, or the Old-World. These were, basically, people of the European "peasant class." They were, in fact, *indentured servants* or serfs, but they did have legal rights under the law and could even work their way out of this servitude. The Indigenous peoples of the New World were the next group targeted as slaves because colonizers needed a large labor force for cultivating/processing of, sugar cane, tobacco, and later "King Cotton." After some time, this idea proved a failure as Indigenous people resisted the newcomers and many fled West. But the primary reason for the failure of this plan was that thousands upon thousands of Indigenous people died off due to many of the maladies that Europeans brought with them to these virgin shores. Europeans at the time, with their crowded cites and terrible hygiene, suffered historic problems with illnesses, including simple things like the common cold and flu. These maladies decimated the indigenous population, along with smallpox and other European-spawned diseases. When the experiment of Indigenous people as slave workers failed, another source of labor was desperately needed. Europeans then looked to steal people from Africa, and thus the all-out assault on the African continent began. This was the genesis of the *African/Atlantic Slave Trade*.

European slavery in the New World was much different from the Old-World slavery. It rained down devastation primarily on ONE people, Black

Africans. Europeans had in effect *racialized slavery* making blacks synonymous with slavery. Through slavery, Africa has been systematically robbed not only of precious resources, but also millions of its people, including, naturally, some of its brightest and strongest. I again remind you the Arab slave trade was flourishing in East Africa. Arabs even castrated thousands of African men because they did not want to chance African men having relations with Arab women. Even the Europeans did not resort to this inhumane practice of castration as a rule. This was not due to any act of kindness; Europeans needed Africans to procreate so new slave populations would be born to work their fields continuously, without interruption. They, it can be said, "planned" on working slaves to death, and then just replace them with fresh bodies, new younger slaves. Yes, newborn babies were designated to be slaves under the law – *only in America!* Slaves were the economic engine to drive their New World's success. Nevertheless, let us not let Arabs off the hook either. It is real, that Arab Muslims are still in the business of enslaving African people *to this day*. As thousands of Africans flee their lands because of famine or war, some Muslim countries are rounding them up at European border crossings and placing them into forced servitude. Look it up, it is heart breaking, and NOTHING is being done to stop it.

Still, the Atlantic European slave trade was distinctly inhumane, and purposely cruel. There were no laws to protect the African slave; in fact, laws were specifically crafted to keep them in slavery. There was simply no way out of this servitude *except* through death or escape. Slavery was an economic plan, a financial institution that powered the America economy, and white Americans into incomparable wealth. Any businessman/woman today knows that, overwhelmingly, the cost of operating any business is the cost of labor. *This is how Europeans and Americans enriched themselves* —at the expense of Black lives— with *zero labor costs*. Slavery had become the *institutional wealth generator* for the United States early economy, particularly for the southern states. Some would argue this fact, but the American Civil War was fought by the southern states primarily for the retention of the slave trade. Please look at Dr. Jeffery Robinson's YouTube Seminar, "*The Truth about the Confederacy.*" Cotton was "King" in the south, cotton picked by slaves created scores of millionaire plantation owners, and European businessmen.

The British eventually banished slavery in their homeland as inhumane in the 1807. This was a hard-fought battle, indeed, as British ports were bursting at the seams with riches and goods created by the slave trade. But slavery did not end in America and the United States until 1865, some 60 years later, as slavery was the driver for the new country's success. Slaves built the U.S. economy and produced wealth beyond belief. It is not surprising to learn that many of the prominent American businesses, and educational institutions of today, built their initial wealth due to the historical utilization of slave labor. Virtually every successful company of the time accumulated riches on the backs of slaves. You can learn actual names of firms or institutions by investigating the information on American history. Some firms/institutions will try to deny these facts, but others have come forward with the truth as an "unfortunate time in American history" and attempt to make some degree of amends when exposed.

Where was religion during this time of slavery? History shows that religion played a huge role in slavery. It is quite disturbing that the two most prominent *religions* in the world, Christianity, and Islam, were both married to and committed to the institution of slavery, and as such have untold amounts of blood on their hands. Both religions stole and or murdered millions of Africans (human beings) in the name of Christianity, or Islam. How do we rationalize this? Was this *God's Will* to enslave and murder blacks? How is it possible to reconcile this horrid, inhumane behavior with the Bible teaching of "*thou shalt not kill?*" Yet, it is okay to massacre millions of blacks and other peoples of color as God's Will? For me, this is deeply troubling.

History shows that Africans did not just lie down though! They waged war, year after year against European and Arab invaders. Yet, these invasions were unending, and to be frank, finally **spears and blades simply could not overcome guns and canons.** It is recorded that one African queen, Nzinga of Angola, fought a 40-year war against the Portuguese (1620 – 1660), before her nation eventually succumbed and signed a peace treaty with Portugal. The assault on Africa was relentless. To add insult to this injury, history records that in most cases, the captive people were *forced to assume* the religion of their captors; refusal to convert risked death. Today, for good or bad, minority peoples of all stripes across the world have been saddled with, and in most cases have since *fully embraced, the religion of their oppressors*, without the consideration of how these new religions would destroy their own culture and history, but they initially had no choice.

It was deeply disheartening for me to watch a YouTube story about African girls being lured to foreign countries for job opportunities. These bogus opportunities were a sham that led to modern slavery situations. What was most striking to me was when one of these poor village moms, was being interviewed about her missing daughter. I could clearly see hanging inside her hut a picture of *White Jesus!!* This image just confirmed that the religious *die has been successfully and thoroughly cast*! Today many Black Christians seek to acknowledge and mitigate this past by the creation of many "African"- themed churches where they can more readily worship in their own best interest without the influence of past European/white domination. Remember, the Roman Catholic Church through Constantine gave us the Bible.

Greeks Study In Egypt

As mentioned, *Alexander* conquered Egypt in 332 BC. After this, Greeks began to flow into Egypt. Numerous scholars came to Egypt to study at the feet of Egyptian priests. Historically, there were thousands of Egyptian priests and scribes whose primary function was to study and learn. They were at the heart of knowledge and spiritual understanding that made Egypt a great civilization. Although Greeks, in modern times, are credited with many scientific advancements in medicine, astrology, geometric and algebraic formulas, these achievements were, in fact, learned from, or in many cases stolen from the works of Egyptian priest/scholars. Remember, the Pyramids (an example of studying the stars, precision engineering and building) and other wondrous works were completed thousands of years before the Greeks and Pythagoras came to Egypt. Again, Greece was not even recognized as a country until 800 BC or so, with Homer's *Iliad* and the *Odyssey*. Rome came on the scene 100 years after Greece, around 700 BC.

After conquering Egypt, Alexander's generals later built the Great Library in his honor. This library became the center of learning of Egypt in the city named after him, Alexandria. It was the largest of its time with thousands of manuscripts and texts from all over the world, including those of Egyptian priests. While Greeks were a learned people, the Romans, who defeated the Greeks later and took over Egypt, also had their scholars and were expert builders, but the Romans were not, generally, of the same intellectual mind as

Greeks. They were more noted for their powerful military. In fact, Dr. Clarke refers to the Romans as THUGS, which is most fitting considering history shows this *decadent society* celebrated and reveled in the practice of men (Gladiators) fighting to their deaths as spectacles of enjoyment, and entertainment for thousands of upper-class revelers. At any rate, this great Alexandrian library burned down in 48 BC., at the hands of the Romans, some believe accidentally. Because of this act, much of the wondrous knowledge of Ancient Egypt, and other immensely valuable writings of the world were lost forever.

Black scholars believe, and repeatedly state that *Egypt was the road map to western civilization* (through the Greeks who, as stated, studied for decades in Egypt). The Greeks were in awe of this ancient land, its Gods, people, and its accomplishments. Just about every prominent Greek poet, mathematician, scientist, philosopher, historian, etc., traveled to Egypt to study and learn from the Egyptian priests. Black Egyptians had a 2,000-year head start on the Greeks in terms of science, astrology, medicine, etc. The emerging Greeks had learned much from the Egyptians which is why they held them in such high esteem. 18th century Danish Naval Captain and explorer Frederic Louis Norden had this to say about Egypt's grandeur in a letter to one of his benefactors after visiting Egypt in 1737-38, **"I have seen the origin of all the sciences. Let them talk to me no more about Rome. Let Greece be silent, if she would not be convinced of having known NOTHING but what she had derived from Egypt! What venerable architecture, what magnificence, what mechanics. What other nation ever had the courage to undertake such works so surprising."** Norden's statement validate that Egypt was a place of magnificence, far ahead of European nations.

Again, the most brilliant of the many notable Egyptian figures was Imhotep—3rd Dynasty (2635 BC) - Figure 2. He was advisor, architect, and physician to Pharoah Djoser. He built the very first pyramid, the Stepped Pyramid. In medicine, Egyptian records state that Imhotep treated more than 200 diseases, among them: 15 of the abdomens, 11 of the bladders, 10 of the rectums, 29 of eyes and 18 of skin. He knew of *blood circulation* 3000 years before it was understood in Europe. He was worshiped as a god for the next 3000 years. There is some indication that Imhotep may have even performed brain surgery, 5,000 years ago! A true genius, two hundred years after his death, he was called the "father of medicine" in Egypt. In fact, the America Medical *"Hip-*

pocratic Oath" is named after a Greek person who studied in Egypt, Hippocrates. He lived 2000 years *after* Imhotep. Hippocrates does, however, praise Asclepius (Greek for Imhotep) in his writings. Pythagoras is another one of the notable Greeks who benefited from studying in Egypt. We all know of the *Pythagorean Theorem, Pythagoras himself studied in Egypt for 23 years.*

There are centuries of Egyptian scholarly writings in tombs, temples, and plentiful writings on papyrus texts and steles, which attest to Imhotep's and other Egyptian priests' knowledge. Many of these writings are still in Egypt, but due to thousands of years of tomb excavations, and tomb robberies the most prominent of these artifacts have been looted, smuggled, and sold to individual collectors and museums around the world. Many of these foreign institutions and collectors refuse to return them even though outside pressure is being turned up on them.

The most prominent of these are listed below:

1. Edwin Smith Papyrus—*Named after a British person who purchased it. This Medical Text describes 48 medical procedures by Imhotep. 1600 BC (written in the 16th and 17th Dynasties).*
2. Rhind Papyrus—*Geometry and Math (1650 BC)*
3. Moscow Papyrus—*Mathematical Texts (1700 BC)*
4. Ebers Papyrus—*Medical procedures (1500 BC)—cardiovascular, dermatology, pulse, dentistry, and gynecology*

The original ancient writings show that early Ethiopians (Greek word for people with burnt skin) migrated all over the Mediterranean and the then-known world. So, while the records confirm Ethiopian migrations, it is also true that as centuries passed, the word *Ethiopian,* as mentioned, became the typical term used by ancient Europeans to describe a person as being *Black,* no matter the African country of origin. Therefore, most of the time, it was not a reference to the country we know today as Ethiopia, but rather simply noting a person with black skin or African.

Diodorus of Sicily: *Ethiopians say that Egyptians are a colony of themselves. The customs of Egyptians are much like Ethiopians. Ethiopians, the Black peoples of Africa, are the 1st of All Men.*

Plato: Zeus was set to feast with Ethiop's faultless men.

Homer's ILLIAD: 1ˢᵗ European literary figure called *Ethiopians righteous men—800 BC.*

Strabo: Greek geographer (63 BC- 24 CE)—*Met with the Noba tribe. He called their country Nubia. Better known as Kush in Ancient times—Today it is Sudan.*

Karl Lipsius, a German scholar: *Discovered a painting in the Tomb of Rameses III 1200 BC with nine figures, but four are of distinct importance to us. They are pointed out to be: Egyptian – A; Indo-Europeans - B: Nubian - C; then Semites – D. Figures **A and C** are pictured as Black figures. "Figure A, where we expected to see an Egyptian, we are presented with an **authentic Negro**."* We spoke of this "Table of Nations" in an earlier chapter.

King Tutankhamen (Boy King): *Tomb found by Howard Carter in 1922. Dated to 1338 BC–1328 BC. He was the son of Pharaoh Akhenaten—and wore the solid gold Death Mask. He was depicted as black in paintings and sculptures.* See Figure 8 (*or search for Tutankhamun on the Internet*).

Regarding the "Table of Nations," in our life's experiences, and historical readings, if we are honest with ourselves, the Egyptians were, without a doubt, a Black race. It is almost unquestionable when looking at the many examples of art from that early era. The "Table of Nations" supports this truth, in as much as the imagery depicts the Egyptian and the African identically. The artist renderings reveal color profiles of men of the day, and in particular, beardless Black men with bald, or close-cropped hair. This is the typical appearance of almost all east African men of the region, i.e., Sudan, Kenya, Ethiopia, etc., to this day. In contrast, almost all men of European, Semitic, or Asian origins of the time are depicted with long hair, and thick beards; some perhaps beardless with wavy hair as the later Greek and Roman art indicate. This point is not meant to be scientific evidence of any sort, nor empirical proof, just my observation.

The world-wide Olympic Games is perhaps the best broad stage where the profiles/silhouettes of numerous African men can be widely viewed, and compared with non-African men, and acknowledge the apparent differences in countries of origin. The similarities to the persons in the "Table of Nations," and countless other examples of Egyptian art depicting Ancient Egyptians, cannot be denied. Although modern day Egyptians are truthfully Arab in origin, not African. Additionally, we know Egyptian priests typically shaved their heads, but can this be said for the entire ancient male Egyptian/African population? Yet the "Table of Nations" clearly depicts the typical Ancient Egyptian man and African man of the time with bald or close-cropped hair. Another fact that catches my eye is the beards of the Pharaohs. It seems to me that if the Pharaohs were European or Semitic, their beards would perhaps not be fake as was the custom, but that of full faced beards as depicted in related images, and art of non-blacks of that era.

Also, please do NOT give any credibility to Hollywood movies that touch on Egyptian History. A recent movie erroneously, and annoyingly paints one of Egypt's most revered characters, Imhotep, as a vengeful villain. This is a total fabrication of the truth! Yet, sadly, this is how millions of modern impressionable young kids will remember him. When recently challenged by black historians about an upcoming movie regarding Egypt that has an overwhelming preference for white actors, the producers/director openly admits that Egyptians were predominantly black but stated that they were more concerned with box office sales than portraying actual historical evidence of black Egyptians. Considering the historic success of the recent *Black Panther* movie, perhaps showing the true black Egyptians would have yielded even greater financial rewards for this movie. KNOW YOUR HISTORY!

Mixing of Races

Africa is an extremely large continent. Due to a cross section of climates & environments, indigenous African people's skin comes in numerous hues of black and brown, depending on their region of origin. Also, thousands of years of war and invasions by neighboring nations caused significant interracial relationships that contributed to additional color variations of mulattos, among others, from the *original* population. Also, conquered kings of other nations often gave daughters and consorts to Egyptian kings as gifts of tribute. In one case, a foreign king is said to have delivered 300 female consorts as a gift to the pharaoh. There are also documented cases of Egyptian raiding parties stealing white women from other cultures as wives or consorts. So, you will likely even see evidence of whites, blond, blue-eyed people at some point in Egyptian history. So, because of this intermingling of races, not all later pharaohs or Egyptian people were necessarily "dark" in skin color hue, but naturally many were possibly brown or yellow, as the foreign infiltrations continued. Today popular figures like singer Beyonce, or actress Viola Davis are both very beautiful "black women," even though their skin tone is vastly different. Still, Herodotus, after many dynasties and thousands of years later, could easily recognize Egyptians as blacks. Nevertheless, the original peoples who migrated from the Sudan, Nubia, Kenya, and Ethiopia to areas north were intensely dark skinned.

Egypt was so dynamic that it is interesting to note that for three thousand years, even invading, conquering nations still sought to embrace its way of life as kings and pharaohs. Yet they failed to carry on greatness in the areas of religion, culture, and building. Whether Hyksos, Assyrians, Persians, or Greeks, they all ruled the nation as pharaohs and continued to try to impact the advancement in art, monuments, and construction, etc., but it was not to be. They could not match the glory of the original Black Egyptians, nor the later Black Nubians/Kushites. In fact, most of these invaders had a hand in destroying many of Egypt's centuries-old monuments as they sought to advance their own greatness, and to diminish that of Egypt. To our delight, Egypt was so vast, that many of these cultural monuments survived, and still exist for our viewing today. It is also worth noting that none of these invading nations ever achieved any real success in southern or Upper Egypt, Nubia/Kush—not even the Romans with their grand military might!

In history, the XXV Dynasty, is, without argument by Europeans today, conceded to be a Black Dynasty. During this period, there were five Black pharaohs who ruled for about one hundred years. These pharaohs are from the nation of Kush (Sudan) who ruled Egypt from approximately 746-653 BC. You may recall the Michael Jackson music video years ago with actor, Eddie Murphy as Pharaoh, and model, Iman, as his queen? This video is an honest portrayal of the Kushite dynasty. The most famous of these Pharaohs was named Taharka. Kushites were an extremely dark-skinned people, so there are no contrary arguments here from European decenters, and we have overwhelming evidence of Kushite rule. There are vast troves of writings, paintings, sculptures, etc., to substantiate this fact. The XXV Dynasty was the last of the golden years of the Egyptian Dynasties and culture. This Dynasty, then, becomes an outlier in European history books as discussed. European scholars try to diminish or reject completely Egypt's original African Pharaohs and influence by calling the XXV Dynasty – **the Dynasty of black Pharaohs.** Remember, the very first "Pharoah" Narmer Menes came from the south to rule over the world's first nation state. There is no proof, ever of white tribes south of Egypt! Only indigenous African peoples.

Egypt's southern neighbors the Kushites on more than one occasion came north to drive out foreign invaders from Egypt. It is recorded history that Kushites drove out/expelled the Hyksos and Assyrian invaders from lower Egypt at different times and restored much of the Egyptian religion and culture during their reign. Ancient Kushites/Nubians are the modern-day Sudanese people. I recall notable author, now deceased, Toni Morrison in one of her novels describing a character's skin tone as "Black," with the added qualifier that he/she was *Sudanese Black*, to emphasize the darkness of the person's skin. So, if the original hue/color of Egyptians' skin was in any way akin to their Sudanese neighbors' skin color, we are talking blue black! Remember, the god Osiris, was called the "Lord of the perfect Black." Yet, Osiris is shown with green skin in many paintings. This is because he was also considered the God of agriculture, rebirth/resurrection, thus the GOD OF LIFE.

Hyksos and Other Outside Invaders

Egypt was a rich land with stockpiles of food, granaries, and vast mineral wealth. They were the envy of all nations in the region and perhaps the world. Naturally as a result, after 1700 BC, it was frequently under siege. The nations listed below, at different times in history, attacked and conquered northern Egypt (lower), so naturally there were instances of interrupted government and religious structure, and a greater occurrence of interracial relationships producing brown/mulatto Egyptians. Yet the Pharaonic system and culture endured for over 3000 years down to Cleopatra. No other ancient, or modern culture can begin to challenge the greatness or duration of the Egyptian's reign. The Hyksos were the first non-African group to conquer and rule Egypt. They ruled lower Egypt for 150 to 200 years. Beginning with the Hyksos, all foreign conquerors sought to rule Egypt in the manner and traditions of the past as pharaohs, including the Ptolemy's (Greeks), but these invaders had no real success in continuing Egypt's cultural greatness.

The Kushites, who were cousins of the Egyptians, eventually came north to defeat, then expel the Hyksos (1580 BC) and were successful in restoring the Egyptian culture and rule, which was much like their own, back to Egypt. It is recorded history that every downturn in Egyptian Dynasties because of invasions, or political turmoil called "intermediate periods," were typically followed by interventions of invading Africans from the south. These Africans (cousins of Egypt) restored cultural, religious connectivity and cultural greatness back to Egypt. This was a reoccurring model, until the final rule of in-digenous Africans in Egypt, with the defeat of the Kushites in 674 BC.

INVADER CHRONOLOGY

Hyksos (Semites): First documented non-Black invaders to conquer Egypt—lower Egypt. They ruled for 150 to 200 years during 15th Dynasty, 1730–1580 BC

Libyans: *From the West —22nd Dynasty 945–817 BC*

Assyrians: *From the East—674 BC*, the sacking of Thebes by the Assyrians marks the beginning of the decline of the Black rule in Egypt.

Persians: *525—404 BC—Cambyses*

Macedonian Greeks: *332–30 BC—Alexander the Great—General Ptolemy I*

Romans: 50 BC to 641 CE—Cleopatra's rule ended in 30 BC

Arabs (Turks): *654 CE to the present*

More on Cleopatra: Her rule was in the 30TH Dynasty. Egypt was in deep decline during her years. Hers was the last of the Egyptian Dynasties. Egypt came to be a Roman province after her death. She was the daughter of Ptolemy VII, a Greek general. Her mother was not a royal but believed to be a consort of African descent. It is reported that the Greek Ptolemies, who ruled as pharaohs, married into Egyptian royalty to better assimilate, and be accepted into the culture, government, religion and rule of the conquered nation. This is a typical practice by invaders seeking some measure of calming, and acceptance. It is folly to think that this conquering army some 300 years later would not have conveniently married and had families with local Egyptian women of royalty, and relationships with the general populations of Egyptian women. Remember, Cleopatra's sister Arsinoe is believed to be of Nubian blood. For a similar modern example of this (on a smaller scale), consider the United State army in Vietnam. Though only there for 10 -20 years thousands of what was termed *"Amerasian"* babies were the result of an occupying army interacting with local women. This both by white, and black American soldiers alike.

Cleopatra herself was very likely what we call today, biracial. She later became mistress of Julius Caesar (producing a son Caesarian), and Marc Antony, hoping they would help to preserve her rule in Egypt. I recently read an article called, "Cleopatra the Greek Pharoah." This article's obvious purpose was to create a white narrative for Cleopatra, as it must have mentioned the "Greek Pharoah" 20 times in a short span. This is akin to calling George Washington the British president of America! Greeks captured Egypt in 332 BC. 300 years later after naturally much Greek and Egyptian in breeding she became pharaoh. Please consider the amount of in breeding here - for 300 years, particularly when Greeks purposely sought to ingrain themselves into the fabric of Egyptian culture.

Alexander the Great (Greek): Conquered Egypt from the Persians in 332 BC—Founded Alexandria, which replaced Memphis as Egypt's most prominent city at that time. His generals built the Great Library at Alexandria that was later burned to the ground by the Romans. Recent theories suggest that the library did not burn down intentionally, but rather there was a fire at least adjacent to the library itself. This theory simply asserts that the library over time lost its stature and just deteriorated and crumbled as the city of Alexandria lost its importance in the ancient world with the rise of Athens and Rome. The Greeks ended up ruling Egypt for three hundred years in total before the Romans took the country.

It is critical to understand the historical dates and time frames to recognize what was happening in Egypt during these various ancient periods. For example, if an archeologist today were to uncover Egyptian tombs dated after 674 BC and later (or during the Ptolemy's rule), then you know right away these tombs of these pharaohs and related mummies are NOT likely to be of Egyptian decent or Black-skinned pharaohs, but rather foreign conquerors still ruling as Pharaohs (*674 BC marked the end of the reign of the XXV Cushite Dynasty Pharaohs and therefore the end of black Rulers in Ancient Egypt*). The same absence of black Pharaohs would also be true during the 200 years of the Hyksos rule and that of the other outside conquering nations listed above.

Destruction of Noses on Sculptures and Monuments

A universal question in the Black community is this: *What about the missing noses on so many Egyptian monuments and statues?* Are these conquering nations responsible for the missing or damaged noses? There is much speculation on this subject. Perhaps modern 18th or 19th century Europeans are responsible for destroying the noses?

The popular story among Blacks, a kind of urban legend, is that European whites who rediscovered Egypt in the 1800s vandalized the monuments, perhaps thinking that by destroying the noses, the world would not recognize that black people originated this highly advanced, ancient civilization. This is certainly plausible! The world during this time was 100 percent embedded in the business of slavery, and in America since 1619. This slave business was built on the idea that Blacks were not human, but savages. It is believed that the removal/damage to the noses was necessary to eliminate any hint that these people, Ancient Egyptians, were *civilized*, intelligent, Black Africans. A few alternative theories for the missing noses are discussed in following paragraphs.

Historians say that Egyptians and peoples of that era held deep beliefs in the spiritual world. It is theorized by academics that Egyptians, and perhaps some of the ancient conquering nations believed that the souls or spirits of people were directly associated with intake of air through the nose. Thus, the dead pharaoh's soul could, in effect, revisit them through their noses, or even be resurrected, enabling them to return to torture or attack the offending conquering persons. To prevent this retribution from occurring, the conquerors destroyed the noses on these monuments to assure that these people in the afterlife (a life force) would not re-emerge through an individual's nose and destroy their offenders. One other thesis is that subsequent pharaohs destroyed/defaced many monuments to discredit their predecessor—to erase them from history.

Another factor in the destruction of many monuments was Christianity. Christian monks and Christianity took hold of Egypt with the Roman conquerors. In the 3rd century CE, these Christians began to establish monasteries in Egypt. Some of these new Christian places of worship (churches) were new construction; others were set up in existing Egyptian/Greek Temples. These obsessed, religious monks were on a mission to destroy as much so-called "*paganism/idolatry*" as they could. This documented behavior was essentially the Christian vandalism of history. They sought to erase all things associated with "pagan" worship, which naturally would have included Egyptian Gods. It is also documented that these Christians destroyed hundreds of existing monuments and temples during their control of Egypt.

Today, Egypt is a majority Arab/Muslim country. In earlier times, even conquering Muslims played a large hand in destroying Egyptian culture and history. It is reported that the smooth limestone finish originally covering the pyramids was demolished, carried away and used to build new Muslim mosques. One Muslim leader, General Amr, after seizing control of Egypt and the city of Alexandria in 640 CE ordered the final destruction of Egypt's educational facilities, libraries, and the University of Alexandria. When his own scholars begged him the retain theses invaluable works, he responded, " if the library contains what is NOT in the Koran it is false. If it contains what is already in the Koran, it is superfluous – BURN IT!

Egypt/Kemet as a unified nation is over 5,000 years old, so there have been ample opportunities for rivals, conquerors, religious zealots, and more recently, racist Europeans to damage and deface these grand images and monuments. What is the truth regarding the noses? *No one can say for sure what happened to the noses!* I am sure debate on this subject will continue for many years to come. Like Diop, I think it is important for us to take the emotion out of any explanation of the missing noses or other Egyptian mysteries, and pursue a more grounded, historically based reasoning for the destruction (if possible). It is true, I might add, that some Greek and Roman statues also have missing or damaged noses, but _not nearly to the extent of Egypt's monuments._ It is important to remember that Egyptian works (in most cases) are thousands of years older than those of the Greek or Romans. Yet, in the end, it is difficult to understand why hundreds of otherwise perfectly preserved sculptures have destroyed noses. This "urban legend" could have some truth to it.

Finally, what about the Sphinx's missing nose? Again, a popular story in the Black community is that Napoleon's troops shot the nose off by firing a cannon ball at it. Diop, while visiting the United States in 1985, gave a speech to a group of Black scholars at Morehouse College. He stated in his lecture that the nose of the Sphinx "fell to the ground" (after all, it is perhaps 10,000 years old—_even stone can lose its continuity over time—my words, not Diop's_). Diop said that the fallen pieces were collected from the ground and now are stored in a British museum. He goes on to say that the Egyptian government could easily request return of the fallen pieces so the nose can be reattached to the grand monument. But the _current_ Egyptians do not want the pieces back, because that nose would be proof of African presence.

There is proof of early sketches of the Sphinx with the nose missing as early as 1737. This drawn by Danish Naval Captain Frederic Louis Norden, in his book _My Travels to Egypt and Nubia_, though published in English years after his death, Napoleon and his army did not come into Egypt until 1798. If this is true, his troops could not have been responsible for the missing nose; they were not on the scene until 60 years later. Another version of the missing nose is an account by an Egyptian Arab scholar written in the 15th century stating that a Suni Muslim man named _Muhammed Saim al dahr_ was responsible for destroying the nose in 1378. Reports are he paid men to disfigure the monument because people were worshiping the Sphinx as a god. This account further states he was executed by local officials because of vandalism of this iconic monument. Finally, it should be noted that the original name of the Sphinx, the Egyptian name, is Her- Em- Akhet . Anthony Browder, in his book _Nile Valley Contributions to Civilization_ points out that the Greeks named it Sphinx, which is from the Greek tragedy _Oedipus Rex_ written by playwright

Sophocles. He states that the Sphinx of this riddle is not a revered image of strength and wisdom of Kemet but is in fact a monstrous figure that devours people who cannot correctly answer the riddle. As such this is not a respectful, or proper moniker for the great monument of Egypt (Kemet).

Egyptian Mythology and the Bible

Religion is, in its simplest form, a *"belief system."* As humans, no matter what our country of origin or culture, most of us seek refuge and solace in a higher power. Today there are thousands of religions around the world, and therefore thousands of *belief systems*. Hundreds of millions of folks around the world worship in their own distinct ways, and they would all contend that their god and worship is the true form of worship. In each religion, the word FAITH is a major determinate, and a constant component in any religion when trying to reconcile its beliefs with science or history. The primary message of most religions, including Christianity, Islam and Judaism is LOVE. Jesus preached love of thy neighbor and to "help the least of your fellow man." If Egypt is the oldest known civilization, then Egypt is the oldest known place of spirituality and worship, existing at least 3000 to 4000 years before Jesus or Mohammed. Ancient Egypt (Kemet) had thousands of priests skilled in spiritual thought, theology, astrology, and science. So *spiritual thought* and spiritual writings existed long before the writings of the Bible or the Koran.

Scholars and worshipers believe that the Bible is one of the greatest books ever written. It is a unique literary accomplishment to be sure. It is extremely important as a moral and spiritual guide. I am sure Muslims would say the same thing about the Koran. As stated earlier, the Bible has 66 books written by at least 60 different people over 1,500 – 2000 years. Are these writings all created under God's holy spirit? Noted Black historian Dr. John Henrik Clarke states, "People say the Bible is the Greatest Story ever told." He then completes his thought by saying, "That is exactly what it is—A STORY." Although the Romans do write of a Christ or Christos, historians say there is simply little documented proof to support important biblical events, or individuals. For religious folks, the word FAITH is the enormous, almost impenetrable, wall blocking intelligent thought and exchange of ideas on the subject. It is an overwhelming controlling factor, dismissing any alternate reasoning or discussion. In certain situations, it can be used to diminish, or totally discard, a person's own intelligence, the very same intelligence that the creator (no matter what you call him/her) endowed within each of us for rational, independent thought. Some would argue that religion is, essentially, a means of control over a population, as Roman Emperor Constantine sought to do.

Again, remembering my college days, a professor in class reasoned that "scientific theory," when presented, is based on years and years of research, perhaps tens of thousands of hours of discovery and validation. Then that theory is subjected to additional years of scrutiny and pointed criticism by outside critics (peer review) in the field before it is accepted by the scientific community as solid science (as with Lucy). With religion, you need NOTHING—no proof, no peer review, no authentication, no documentation, no fossil finds—all you need is that one word, "FAITH." If you dare question Bible or Quran's writings, your faith is questioned, and you can be seen as a danger, even a heretic, by your congregation. *At this point, let me be a bit provocative when it comes to Religion.* How does one rectify Adam and Eve (Biblical creation) with the evidence of thousands of bones and fossil finds of at least 20 early hominin species discovered by science, and the fact that the first humans originated in Africa? People of faith totally dismiss this. Do we trust science only when it is convenient? Do your research!

Also, as mentioned, a study of the Bible compared to Ancient Egyptian texts reveal that many biblical events and stories are just a retelling (and whitening) of Egyptian religious and mythological stories. The most prominent of these being the Virgin Birth, the Resurrection, and the Trinity.

> **Pre-Dynastic Trinity:** Religion and Mythology—Ausar, Auset, and Heru (4400 BC)
>
> **Dynastic Trinity:** Osiris, Isis, and Horus
>
> **Christian Trinity:** Father, Son, and the Holy Spirit

The Virgin Birth Story of the Bible (Mary, the Holy Spirit and Jesus) is taken from the above Pre-Dynastic Egyptian mythological story documented thousands of years before the Bible existed. In this story, King Ausar married Auset; his brother Set, jealous for power, killed Ausar and cut his body into 14 pieces, spreading the parts around the land. Ausar and Auset had not yet consummated their marriage before his death. The story goes that Auset went searching about the land and found Ausar's body parts (except for his penis, which was reportedly thrown in the Nile and eaten by a crocodile). She then put his body back together, wrapping it as a mummy (considered Egypt's first mummy). Later, Ausar's spirit came to her in the night, and she became pregnant, giving birth to a son, Heru. *This Egyptian story is thousands of years before the Bible's Virgin Birth story.* The famous Egyptian Obelisk is a representation of this missing penis. It stands as a symbol of resurrection/regeneration and life and can be found in cities around the world.

As stated, this may be hard for avid peoples of faith to accept these historic accounts like the Trinity. It is easy enough to research the Egyptian works to verify these facts. Please review the simple timeline section earlier in this paper. The Bible was written thousands of years *after* Ancient Egypt's glory days.

Readers of faith should ask themselves a couple of very simple questions. Why are there no writings by the Greeks and Romans, or any documentation in Egyptian tombs or papyrus writings of the time, supporting biblical accounts? 1) *Why are Moses, Jesus or other biblical events and characters not mentioned in historical writings, by the Egyptians, Greeks, or Romans, but mentioned ONLY in the Bible? 2) Certainly, an EXODUS of 600,000 (if you take into consideration women and children, the totals are easily over 1 million) Jews from Egypt, a PARTING of the Red Sea, Jesus' walking on water, etc., would have been "front page news" so to speak, all over the known world.* Common reasoning tells me that these and other amazing biblical events would have generated a multitude of documentation in records and recitals by historians and scholars of that time! Remember, the Egyptian priests were prolific writers, logging all types of relevant events on Papyrus. Again, remove the emotion, ask yourselves practical questions.

Regarding God, C.F. Volney in his book *The Ruins of Empires* argues religious worship can be attributed to the physical elements of nature. Since early man could not explain, the wind, the sun, etc., he began to look at these as personification of a higher being. Volney states, "In a word, all the theological dogmas on the origin of the world, the nature of God, the revelation of his laws, the manifestation of his person are known to be only figurative and emblematical accounts of the motion of the heavenly bodies, the very idea of a God… is nothing but the physical powers of the universe. So that god is sometimes the wind, the fire, the water, all the elements, the sun, the stars, the moon, the planets the total universe sometimes abstract metaphysical qualities." It is clear, that his life was not rooted in religion, but grounded by daily practical observations.

Thus, ancient peoples as the Egyptians, began to honor/worship these powerful unseen forces as gods. They attached different names to them; Hapi the Nile god, Aton the Sun God, Sobek the Crocodile headed God, Shu the god of air, etc., etc.

Also, the Bible, perhaps unintentionally, lays the groundwork for some very impactful racial division, along color lines. At minimum it fuels the conversation among Christians, Muslims, and Jews as an explanation for black skin, that reason, being that blacks are *inferior and designated to be slaves*. Genesis 9:20 states that Noah's son Ham, and his lineage (Canaan) would be cursed. This passage was originally thought to justify Canaanites being *subjugated* to the Israelites, but centuries later, it has been used by a segment of the worlds' religious European community to suggest Black's inferiority through black skin (Ham's curse). Flavius Josephus, Roman-Jewish historian, states "Ham's descendants populated Egypt," the Bible also refers to Egypt as the "Land of Ham." These references on the positive side, supports the argument that Ancient Egyptians were black – the Bible tells us so! But really, do not the early Greeks make a very common-sense observation on Blacks or Ethiopians? They simply come from or originated in a place in antiquity where the sun burnt their skin, modern science supports this.

The Introduction and Impact of the European

The emergence of the European (whites) was a game changer for peoples of color around the world. This was a different kind of people. Diop's theorizes that the unparalleled ruthless, bloodletting and dominance seeking actions of the European on the world's people of color can perhaps be traced back to his beginnings. Born in an unforgiving frozen, barren landscape (the ice age) , enduring the harsh elements for thousands of years in the daily fight to stay alive, perhaps produced an aggressive survival-first conditioned people, a vicious take-whatever-you-need mentality, with no boundaries or consideration for the wellbeing of others—only the strongest will survive. To understand the social and psychological construct to survive in these conditions, their need to utilize violence to dominate other clans/tribes of people in this type of environment is, I am sure, an entire subject of study of its own.

We have established that our ancestors in Africa and Egypt had successful grand civilizations for thousands of years. Egypt was clearly an advanced society admired by the ancient world and the modern world alike before the appearance of the Europeans. The ancient Greeks were in awe of this accomplished black race of people, calling them "beautiful, and faultless." Egyptians were quite capable of worshipping the creator according to their own tradition and culture, specifically the teachings of MAAT in Egypt. The teachings of *resurrection*, the transition to the spirit world or afterlife, the *Virgin Birth*, the belief in *One God*, are all *original* Ancient Egyptian spiritual values.

History shows the modern Europeans appeared in Africa and, basically, murdered millions upon millions of black people, not savages, but our ancestors! Then they went about the systematic task of destroying black culture and worship, finally forcing their religion upon blacks with such ferocity that our ancestors had to accept their worship, or death.

MAAT represented 42 principals/ideals enacted to inspire and establish an orderly Egyptian society. These ideals date back to the time of Narmer Menes and can be found in the *Papyrus of Ani*, a text from the *Egyptian Book of the Dead*. They are personified by MAAT, the Ancient Egyptian Goddess of Truth, Justice, and Order and were fundamental to the teachings of spiritual harmony and balance. A quick sampling of these pronouncements is *1) I have not committed sin, 2) I have not stolen, 3) I have not slain men or women, etc., etc.* The Soul of the deceased person must honestly declare that he/she has lived up to these standards when standing for judgment before being allowed entering the afterlife.

Please take notice, unlike the Ten Commandments, which say "DO NOT" violate these laws, Egyptian citizens seeking approval to enter the afterlife must pronounce, "I HAVE NOT" committed these violations of MAAT. MAAT lists 42 laws or *Negative Confessions* created as far back in history as 2900 BC, thousands of years before Europeans came to Egypt, before Christianity, before a Bible, or persons called Jesus or Mohammed! In fact, scholars believe that Bible writers borrowed from MAAT to form the Biblical "10 Commandments."

Blacks have since become one of the most dedicated religious people of the world, praying to that same God(s) and religion(s) that made them slaves; slaves to those who Dr. Clarke stated, "committed genocide against us, the greatest crime against a people in the history of the world." Seriously, I ask: how did Christianity or Islam work out for our ancestors?

Still in truth, killing and bloodletting, sad to say, has been an integral part of human existence from time immemorial. In church, to help us young kids remember the Biblical story of Cain and Able, we were taught this *cute teaching phrase* - "Cain killed Able, who was unable with a Cane." So, killing and death are not new. Every country has its own dark history of wars and violence, and atrocities, but I do not believe anyone could have imagined the total wholesale aggression and destructive nature of the people who came out of the European continent. Perhaps a more truthful/honest education in American schools could include dissecting historical data, including an attempt to explain why the Europeans were the most brutal, domination-seeking people in the history of the world. Why have they killed millions upon millions of people worldwide to establish what is really white supremacy?

Much of this bloodletting occurred in the name of religion and was unleashed in every country unto which they set foot! What causes white people to kill massive amounts of wildlife to the point of extinction—like the American Bison? Millions were reduced to a few hundred because of the European killing spree during their migration westward, although history states a large percentage were killed just to deny Native Americans of a consistent food source. These people shot bison from trains for fun. Today they systematically hunt and kill majestic wildlife—for SPORT? Then cut-off and hang the heads on their living room walls as proud trophies? This, while all other people on earth over thousands of years have sought to live in harmony with the land and take animal lives (God's creatures) only for sustenance or safety. Education is needed!

Dr. Frances Cress Welsing (1935–2016), a noted Black physical psychologist and human behavior professional, in her book the *ISIS Papers* takes an in-depth look at the impacts of skin color, the psyche and history of the white race. She presents her theory of the European (whites) and their dismissive relationship to nonwhites worldwide. She delves deep into psychoanalytical reasons and tries to "decode" this type of superior behavior. She deals with behaviors of the Europeans such as envy (color envy) and narcissism, and then breaks them down by describing the many important symbols of the *subconscious mind* that are imbedded in Europeans regarding skin color, which perhaps speaks to their need to impose their idea of "purity" and thus to force their will on other peoples. It is truthfully a controversial set of theories, yet her work is not to be dismissed and deserves a close look.

Putting science and psychology aside, the most obvious reason for white aggression is the *numbers game*. Whites perhaps make up about 15-20 percent of the entire world population; various peoples of color make up the other 75-80 percent. Dr. Welsing believes that whites live in ultimate fear. They believe they *must* dominate the world's people of color under their thumb out of a distinct fear of being physically overrun/pushed aside. Today this belief has a specific name coined by whites – "The Replacement Theory." Whites fear being "replaced" both politically and economically by non-whites.

In early America, it was common for slaves to outnumber white slave masters and their families on plantations, and in the community. To keep slaves in line, and maintain control, the slave master was unusually brutal and cruel, and showed no hesitancy in whipping, dismembering, or killing slaves, making it clear to others what the consequences of disobedience would bring. Still, there were many historically documented slave rebellions as this domination could not prevent people from seeking their natural birthright of freedom. Many preferred death to bondage, and servitude. Just as with the plantation slave owners, modern politicians (conservatives) of all Eurocentric nations are very aware that they, indeed, are the *real minority peoples* on the earth.

The *Color Envy* point sounds trivial and unimportant, even laughable on the surface, until taking a closer look. White skin, as we have discussed, is a deficiency, deficient of the important molecule/component of melanin, and as a result, their skin is pale and, to many, unattractive, not to mention the problem of susceptibility to dangerous UV ray damage. *This cannot be trivialized!* Millions of white people will sit/lay hours upon hours out in the sun—at risk of skin cancer, and possible DEATH—*while seeking a darker, more attractive hue to their colorless skin.* Millions have died over the years (of skin cancer) as a result. In America alone, there is a multibillion-dollar cosmetic industry that provides sunscreen and other medical remedies for the white population, as sunbathing is an *unstoppable past-time* at beaches, backyards, and now tanning salons as whites are determined to garner a darker, more beautiful skin color. It is clear here that the word *envy* is indeed appropriate. Also, we have all heard the phrase growing up in black communities that *"black don't crack."* This, common phrase is used to describe the youthful vitality and appearance of black skin which, of course, is due to the high melanin content. It is estimated by some accounts that a black person's skin will hold its youth / vitality as much 10 years longer than a white person's skin.

It is a fact that European men are afraid, even paranoid, with the thought of Black men being with white women. The history of lynching and castrations of Black men is well documented throughout American history. What kind of hate causes a "civilized" people to *hang, castrate and then finally burn the body of another human being* to the cheers of thousands of onlookers? This is no 1619 Project - this is, in fact, American History - and very much akin *to the Roman citizens cheering death at the Colosseum (though not racially motivated) - just indiscriminate bloodletting* . To Romans, it was, sad to say – sport; but for white Americans, it was hatred of, in their eyes, the *sub-human* black man. Of these 18th and 19th century American throngs (at times thousands of cheering on-lookers of lynching's), how many of them were laborers, teachers, property owners, businessmen, politicians, lawyers, policemen, store owners, judges, etc.? This conglomeration of white Americans made up the typical community. As such, it is only natural that a large segment of the white population today, as part of this modern *typical community*, still perpetuates these same attitudes and continue to reveal themselves as racists today. A significant percentage of these same "*fine Americans—God-fearing Christians*" are woven into the fabric of the entire American system of life—at every level. Thus, Blacks are correct to point out that there exists "*systematic racism*" throughout this society—there is no question!

We spoke earlier of *miseducation*. The average white person has also been miseducated to believe that they are a superior race, chosen to subjugate all others based on their skin color. They see blacks as lazy, inferior, and thus inherently underachievers. The intense racial divide that exists in America and the world is a *by-product* of this miseducation. Perhaps this embedded turmoil could be mitigated *to some degree* by a revamped educational system throughout the country; a system that includes a middle and high school curriculum that teaches the truth of the Nile Valley civilization and African greatness.

I recall an advanced English writing class I attended many years ago. The subject was Ethnic Writers, which meant we read books by people of color, i.e., Black authors, Chinese, Asian authors, Mexican and American Indian authors. We read several compositions and wrote papers on each. I have read many books on the pain of Black people, but it was an awakening to learn just how deeply the white man had injured these other people of color, *not more than blacks by any stretch of the imagination*, but to hear their experiences in their words was stunning. We all know, generally, of the far-reaching, devastating pain wreaked by Europeans, but to read the shocking words of these various writers, brown, yellow, and red people was indeed mind-blowing and painful. You learn quickly of the kinship that all people of color have in the experience of death and genocide due to the advancement of the "white power" culture.

Therefore, it is pure ignorance for any person of color to look down their noses at another person of color, or tell them to get out, or go back to their own country, as has recently been occurring with our Chinese brothers and sisters because of Covid. We are all victims in history of the European's unbridled need to dominate all other human beings of color. Even the revolutionary group of the sixties and seventies, the Black Panthers Party changed their powerful slogan of "Black Power" to the even more powerful recital of "Power to the People," which was more inclusive of other wronged peoples. Still, the human condition, and our own cupidity continues to foster racism across all nationalities. Therefore, it is no shock to see blacks, as the least acceptable of all so called "minority groups." A statement generally known among blacks reflects the experience of life among the world's people, it goes, "If you are white - you are right, if you are brown - stick around, if you are black - get back." Therefore, from birth, Blacks do not expect an easy road in life for us or our children, we need to be ready for the challenge. We teach our children this every day. Still, with centuries of disrespect, pain, and millions of deaths, I personally do not know a single black person who does not embrace and celebrate his/her blackness, or who would rather be white! Although there's always a few feeble-minded blacks seeking white acceptance, like Michael Jackson, or Sammy Sosa who have actually used chemicals to whiten their skin.

It just so happens that a young white man trying to fulfill his English writing requirement had the misfortune (or maybe good fortune) of signing up for this class. He got an ear full every single day on how evil his people were. They had murdered and/or mistreated people of color from all groups throughout the entire globe. It got so bad that one day he just blurted out, "So what am I – the Devil?"

The class just looked at him and one person responded – "The truth hurts, right?" These writers are speaking the truth, the truth of their ancestors. I am sure this young man knew of slavery, and the plight of America's indigenous people, but not the in-depth tearful accounting as these authors described in their books. He had never heard the *truth* of the overwhelming pain and sorrow experienced by the peoples who literally built this country, the pain inflicted by the brutal acts of his people to dominate other cultures.

This young man represents the ignorance of most whites in the U.S., and around the world who, just like us – have been miseducated and have no knowledge of real, accurate history; only the history written to the glory, benefit, and superiority of his people - European / whites. As mentioned earlier, a new course of teaching/learning is needed. This would help set the record straight and perhaps generate new attitudes of brotherhood around the world. Black folks are not seeking retribution for past bloodshed - only a fair, even playing field moving forward in terms of opportunity, education, jobs, and human rights. It is just that simple, although there is legitimate conversation to be had on reparations.

White folks should know that they came from US. They are a mutated version of Black people. This knowledge would hopefully dispel the savage, no-history lies that have proliferated in history books for hundreds of years regarding Blacks. But this is a pipe dream, as racist politicians and their fervent supporters will never let this happen. They will not let the truth be told in a systematic, accurate way. As proof, look at the current hysteria by racist whites surrounding the proposed "1619 Project," which has been used to generate panic and to energize whites around a continued white protectionist outlook in this country. They fearfully perceive the end of "their power scenario" at the hands of their dreaded *Replacement Theory* by blacks. A popular modern educator on racial bias is Jane Elliot. She is a white woman who is an "in your face" bold truth teller. She is very controversial, not only for her message, but because of her hard-hitting delivery of this message toward the white race. Please look up her work on her "blue eyes/brown eyes" experiment, a study of bias and the resulting brutal impacts/reaction of ordinary white people to discriminatory treatment based solely on blue eyed persons vs brown eyed persons.

Conclusion

The previous pages are only a brief, simplified review of my readings of Ancient Egypt and African/Black history. I may have gotten some of the *exact dates* wrong, and a few details may have changed because things tend to change with *new* archeological/scientific finds. Overall, though, this information is on point. The story of Ancient Egypt (Kemet) is long and extremely complicated, but the facts are there for anyone who wishes to examine them. Years ago, 5,000 - 10,000 years, an advanced civilization existed in Africa along the Nile River. It thrived and left us a remarkable record of their history (in stone and papyrus) for us to cherish. It was so advanced that one section of modern scholars still believe that *aliens* must have built the pyramids. They feel that humans of that time could not possibly have constructed such large grand structures. The proof of this history is vast, and we have the records and structures as proof down to our day. They even tell fantastical stories of bones found of "giants," suggesting they must have built the pyramids.

It truly angers me when I see or hear current Egyptians basking in the glory of Ancient Egypt. I am immediately reminded of Dr. Van Sertima's words, *"They did not have a Damn thing to do with Ancient Egypt!"* They are Arabs, they had no early history or culture of building, and did not come into and conquer Egypt until 654 CE, a full 2,000 years after the Great Pyramids were built!

Egypt is Africa! The Europeans have tried to steal the accomplishments and the glory of Ancient Egypt from black Africans, to make it their own. It is blatant racism to put forth the lie that Egyptians were not Black during the predominate periods of the Dynasties. Even the bible tells us that Egypt was the Land of Ham, Diop also proves this. The idea that Black people had no hand in the building, science, cultural development, religion, and government of Egypt is, to be blunt, is laughable.

Remember, Malcolm told us, "We've been lied to." Kemet—the original name of the land, was translated as the "land of the Blacks" for 3000 years. It only became "Egypt" after the Greeks (Alexander) conquered it, which was very late in the Dynastic history. History shows the people there referred to themselves as KMT—the negroes. Egyptian Hieroglyphic writings for *"kmt"* reveals a person, or persons standing next to a piece of charcoal.

Many European scholars would have you believe that Black people had nothing to do with Egypt. They have promoted for hundreds of years that the term "Black Land" really means *Black Soil*—NOT *Black people*. This is a shell game! Let's throw some ridiculous explanation out there. If we repeat it enough, much like our recently impeached and defeated former President Donald Trump does, it will take hold and become TRUTH. This seems to be their strategy; the primary argument that they promote and cling to is this notion of *Black Soil*, but this lie is now crumbling!

The Nile Valley floods yearly , because of the water coming down from the Great Lakes of the Rift Valley and mountains of Ethiopia/Uganda. This yearly flood accounts for Egypt's historical success with agriculture because of the new rich topsoil deposited annually by these floods. The White Nile originates 4,162 meters upstream (south) from Cairo in Uganda. The Blue Nile begins in Ethiopia. From an elevation of 1840 meters, the White Nile converges with the Blue Nile near Khartoum in the Sudan about 1500 mile later. Then, the grand river thunders downwards as its travels north through the Sudan delivering life sustaining waters to Egypt, finally dropping to EL 0.0 at sea level as it reaches the city of Alexandria and the Mediterranean Sea. This annual replenishment of new rich dark soil is then conveniently misinterpreted and used for the European disingenuous argument for the term "Black Land." However, this rich soil was primarily along the corridor of the Nile River, not throughout the entire country. It is important that our ancestors left us with thousands of examples of Black images throughout the land, as well as writings and commentary from Egyptian, Greek, Arab, and Roman writers.

It is inconceivable that Blacks would be totally absent from this culture! This is AFRICA! European scholars will concoct all kinds of excuses to discount Black's legitimate participation in Dynastic Egypt. If you point to ancient works of art that depict Black Egyptians and pharaohs, they say, *"Well, the different colors are actually religious meanings."* In the cases of the many Black mummies, they say, *"They are black because the resin used in the mummification process turns them black."* They will turn all sorts of flips and flops to distort the fundamental roles Blacks played throughout Egyptian society.

One noted French scholar (Champollion the younger) had the audacity to say, *"Just because a person has Black skin, and wooly hair does not make him African."*—WTF! His brother, by the way (Jean Francois Champollion), is the person who was given credit for deciphering the hieroglyphics on the Rosetta stone twenty-five years after its discovery. Still, this is how desperate Europeans were - NOT to give credit to Black Africans!

Modern doubters still will point to Rameses II's mummy and say he had straight, red hair so he could not have been black. <u>Well, Egyptian Priest Manetho (300 BCE), writing the *History of Egypt* in Greek (Aegyptiaca) stated that Egyptians killed and burned red-headed men (as cursed), and scattered their ashes with fans.</u> This is firsthand, from an actual Ancient Egyptian priest! We have already shown that black Africans/Egyptians came with various hues of skin color and hair textures. In addition, wouldn't it be the case that Rameses II at death (ninety-seven years old) would have had gray/white hair, not red, or blond? Wouldn't this be more plausible? What is really the truth? Some white/European scholars today say that the new wave of Black *Afrocentricity* is wrongfully painting Egypt as Black to advance Blacks' own Afrocentric movement. I say we are fortunate to have Black scholars like Diop, Van Sertima, Clarke, and Browder to tell us and the world the truth. Yet, it is heartwarming today to know that numerous newly educated 21st century white scholars themselves are now retelling the truth of an African Egypt.

Anthony Browder has been to Egypt over sixty times. His group is the *ONLY Black-funded and operated "archeological dig" in Egypt—in history!* This "Dig" is of an Egyptian priest's tomb. This tomb belongs to the Kushite XXV Dynasty. The Dig and tomb restoration he calls the *Asa Restoration Project*, in respect and remembrance of another noted Black scholar, Asa Hilliard. This

"Dig" is in progress at this very moment. I traveled with his group the summer of 2022 to Egypt and saw the wonders of Egypt with my own eyes – although Browder's dig was not available to the public during our visit. Still, this was an immensely emotionally and intellectually rewarding trip.

Hopefully, just like the rewriting of the Columbus story, continued study and persistent truth-telling by Black and white scholars alike will reveal and validate the immeasurable influences of Black Africans at the highest levels of Egyptian and African Civilizations, as well as their contributions world-wide. We must seek to enrich ourselves by learning—correctly—and then teaching our children about our own amazing history. I invite anyone reading this book to do your own investigation. If you do not agree with what I have presented in these pages, do your own work. Do the research; you will have an awakening.

Today, in many ways, a large percentage of our Black youth are lost, and nowhere near meeting their collective potential. A large segment is wrapped up in drugs, violence, etc. They emulate the questionable behavior of popular characters seen in movies and on TV. This is true for both young Black men and Black women. Malcom told us that we come from a Nation of "Kings and Queens," yet it is truly distressing that many of our young men *cavalierly and routinely* refer to our women as "bitches and whores," with many of these same women also referring to their sisters in the same manner, with a boldness and warped bravado that is bewildering!

In Africa and Egypt black women were highly respected, yes many were Queens, and priestesses but all critical to the successful African cultures. Has the European destroyed that sacred respected union of the black family to where it is irreparably damaged? Have we have lost our moral compass, and greatness that our ancestors spent thousands of years crafting for us? Yes, we have been damaged by the European, but we have not been defeated. We must recapturer, rediscover our compass to greatness.

The American *white run* judicial system was designed to incarcerate as many of our young Blacks, and other peoples of color as possible. In fact, history shows that modern police departments are an extension or off-shoot of the *slave catcher groups* authorized by southern plantation owners to lock up or bring back runaway slaves—their property. As a result, a racist slave-catching attitude permeates in white law enforcement to keep prisons filled with our

Black youth. Black author Michelle Alexander does an excellent job of dissecting this racist justice system in her book, *The New Jim Crow*.

Black scholars believe that it is vital for our young folks to learn the true history of Kemet and the Nile Valley. Our young people must understand and know that they come from one of most accomplished people to ever walk this earth—their African/Egyptian ancestors.

Our young have been thoroughly miseducated to think that our history *started* with slavery, that we have no history other than that—that we, as a people, come from savages. Black people have been "spoon fed" a false depiction of our history by Europeans, in their books, and in their movies. Our history did not start with slavery. Slavery of our proud ancestors was the result of naked European aggression and greed, thus the devastation of the African continent, and its peoples.

On being "spoon fed" I'd like to share a quick story. A good friend was in a relationship with a woman who constantly took advantage of him. She was beautiful, yet deceitful, and untrustworthy even as he lavished her with money, gifts, trips, vacations, etc. He would often complain to me, and those close to him how she lied, how she treated him badly, etc. Family and friends would have to constantly listen to his whining. Finally, his mother (an elderly woman) was fed up listening to him fret about his situation. One day, she lit into him with these words: ***"Boy, you don't let nobody feed you – SHIT WITH A SPOON!"*** This was an angry, yet profound statement. Leave it to our elders to speak the unfiltered truth.

There is a deeply relevant message here that can easily be correlated with our black history. The European has miseducated us, lied to us, slaughtered us by the millions, and enslaved us. He then devised a slick campaign to whitewash our true history. He has programmed and mislead us for generations as to our true history. He has been feeding us the European version of history. In other words, to maintain his white supremacist position, he has been symbolically feeding Blacks **"shit with a spoon"** for hundreds of years. As free thinkers, we must always question and examine what modern white society is "feeding us" or trying to feed us in terms of education and history. The truth is that blacks have been fed lie after lie after lie for hundreds of years. However, recent decades show how intelligently and forcefully our black scholars have been pushing away from their table of lies. We have been rejecting their poison. We refuse to be "spoon fed" any longer.

Truth telling about our Black ancestors is paramount. For the millions of our Black youth, it is believed that by knowing and internalizing these truths of Kemet, the real African history, would encourage them to remember and restore the legacy of their ancestors with pride, and to apply themselves, to honor life, and give RISE to the high place that our ancestors lived before us. Donny Hathaway says in one his less popular songs that, "***Being young, gifted and Black - Is where it's at***." I recently discovered that Nina Simone originally wrote and performed that song - celebrating the richness of Black artistic talent. Black leaders and parents should constantly reaffirm and celebrate this statement with their young, at home and in the classrooms, and inspire them to remember and emulate the richness of their ancestors' past. The creativity is within them; the intelligence is within them. It is their legacy! Far too many of our young folks, aspire to be thugs! The "slave catching" police of the day are ready and willing to build more jails to incarcerate them. We must reverse this trend.

At the end of this work, one thing is still extremely bothersome to me. It has been consistent in my short study and readings that Black scholars routinely detail or cite the writings of European scholars, ancient and current. I may be missing something here, but I have yet to see any European scholar give ANY historical value or credit to the writings or works of *any* Black scholar—NOT even to Diop! Only the UNESCO work credits Diop and Obenga for their work on Africa and Egypt as extremely well researched. Today still, the European system cannot let go of its racist outlook and acknowledge the many remarkable works of Diop and other Black scholars. When have you last seen a main stream European college's syllabus include works by black scholars? Yet, modern historian, Robert Bauval's popular book, *Black Genesis*, does recognize and credit Diop's research and work. Bauval devotes almost an entire chapter to Diop and refers to his *melanin* study and techniques as the **"Silver Bullett"**- capable of finally settling the dispute of skin color once and for all. But we know the requested skin (one milliliter) for sampling from the mummified remains of the great Pharaohs were never provided by Egyptian authorities.

Remember my comments earlier on the professor who said, "We just don't know much about Africa?" Most white educators do not want to know black studies, or they will skew what they learn to discredit black intellectuals. After this writing, it is even more clear to me, and by now it should be clear to you, that we MUST seek out the works of our own Black historians, scientists, and archeologist along with creditable Europeans to get a detailed, truthful telling of our story. Racist Europeans have had a specific goal in mind—*to discredit Blacks at every opportunity.* Diop believed it is imperative that we encourage our young Black men and women to study engineering, science, anthropology, paleoanthropology, etc. Then we will be better equipped tell our own truthful story of history and greatness.

Finally, regarding Kemet, I must share the words of French Historian C. F. Volney. While traveling through Egypt in 1783, he observed the physical traits of the Egyptians. He said they had *"bloated face, puffed eyes and flat nose—exactly the appearance of the Sphinx."* It was clear to him that these people were of African descent. So now, he knew someone, ***"Obviously not the Europeans nor the Greeks of Ancient times, but someone much older, had studied the universe and mastered many of its deepest secrets."*** He was able to research and review these great works and the brilliant history of Kemet. C. F. Volney was not hesitant to give the deserved credit for these accomplishments to Blacks.

He lived during the period of the thriving Atlantic Slave Trade and was moved to comment on the total absurdity of the European treatment of Blacks. This treatment led him to write the following about Ancient Egypt in relation to Blacks in his classic work, *"Ruins of Empires."*

"…There, a people, now forgotten, discovered, while others were yet barbarians, the elements of the arts and sciences, A race of men now rejected from society for their sable skin and frizzled hair, founded on the study of the laws of nature, those civil and religious systems which still govern the universe."

Also,

"… That this race of Blacks who nowadays are the slaves and objects of our scorn is the very one to which we owe our arts, our sciences and even the use of the spoken word: and finally recollected that it in the midst of the people claiming to be the greatest friends of liberty and humanity that the most barbarous of enslavements have been sanctioned, and the questions raised as to whether Black men have brains of the same quality as those white men!"

IF YOU DIDN'T KNOW—NOW…. YOU KNOW!

Reference Reading

Christopher Columbus and the African Holocaust—Dr. John Henrik Clarke
African Origin of Civilization, Myth or Reality—Dr. C. A. Diop
Civilization or Barbarism—Dr. C. A. Diop
Egypt Revisited—Various Essays, edited Dr. Ivan Van Sertima
Great African Thinkers—Various Essays, edited by Dr. Ivan Van Sertima
    and L. O. Williams
They came before Columbus—Dr. Ivan Van Sertima
Moses and Monotheism—Sigmund Freud
General History of Africa Vol. II (UNESCO) —James Curry
Wonderful Ethiopians of Ancient Cushite Empire—Drusilla Dundee Houston
From the Browder File—Anthony T. Browder
The Nile Valley contributions to Civilization – Anthony T. Browder
Lucy, The Beginnings of Mankind—Donald Johanson
Ruins of Empires—C.F. Volney
Dr. Ben Josef Ben Jochannan—The Myth of Genesis and Exodus
The ISIS Papers—Frances Cress Welsing
Blacks in Antiquity—Frank R. Snowden Jr.
My Global Search of the African Presence – Ronoko Rashidi
Travels to Egypt and Nubia – Frederic Louis Norden
The New Jim Crow – Michelle Alexander
Black Genesis – Robert Bauval & Thomas Brophy

YOUTUBE—WEBINARS/SYMPOSIUMS/ONLINE LECTURES

Dr. John Henrik Clarke—A Great and Mighty Walk

Dr. Nina Jablonski—The Evolution and Meaning of Skin Color

Dr. Rebeca Futo Kennedy—Civilizations in Antiquity, Herodotus on Ancient Africa

Dr. Jeffery Robinson—The Truth about the Confederacy

Dr. Jane Elliot – Blue Eyes - Brown Eyes.

Dr. Richard Ehret – The Africanity of Ancient Egypt

Micheal T. Robinson – TEDx Talk "The Hamitic Philosophy"